ENTERTAINING IN THE LIGHT STYLE

ENTERTAINING
IN THE LIGHT STYLE

LOU SEIBERT
PAPPAS

Drawings by
Veronica di Rosa

101 PRODUCTIONS   SAN FRANCISCO

Printed and bound in the United States of America.

Distributed to the book trade in the United States
by Charles Scribner's Sons, New York.

Published by 101 Productions
834 Mission Street
San Francisco, California 94103

1 3 5 7 9 11 13 15 17 19 KP 20 18 16 14 12 8 6 4 2

Library of Congress Cataloging in Publication Data

Pappas, Lou Seibert.
    Entertaining in the light style.

    Includes index.
    1. Entertaining.   2. Menus.   3. Cookery.
International.   I. Title.
TX731.P2917   1982   642'.4   82-14193
ISBN 0-89286-207-6

Contents

Introduction

Entertaining is staging a comeback, but in a new, contemporary style. Light, fresh fare with an innovative ethnic touch is the keynote of communal feasting today. The joys of sharing one of life's greatest, yet simplest pleasures—eating—are being renewed with a bit of drama borrowed from the world's kitchens.

Food lovers everywhere are embracing a lighter, leaner cuisine. The spotlight on healthy living is shaping our culinary fashion. Suddenly less is more. By stripping away superfluous salt, sugar, and fats, flavors are heightened. In tandem, the emphasis is on seasonal bounty, swiftly prepared and artistically presented.

Simplicity is the key to a joyous table today. Naturally this favored dining concept carries over when entertaining. Guests appreciate a streamlined repertoire. No longer need they be satiated with overabundance.

Celebrating the cuisines of the world is a rewarding way to stage a party. Guests delight in the surprise of new flavors. Increased travel has educated taste buds to embrace a worldly sphere. And bounteous markets bring the ethnic and exotic foods within easy reach. Plus, these worldly classics tend to be thrifty, pleasing the cost-conscious party planner.

The notion of entertaining in a make-ahead fashion is no longer the only way. Time is at a premium. With a majority of women working, the genie has fled from the kitchen and spare hours for advance preparation are often nonexistent. By necessity, many party menus have become cooperative and even spontaneous. Spouses or companions may work in tandem, dovetailing culinary chores. Guests may each bring a course for a prearranged menu or lend a hand on the spot. Guests pitching in to chop, roll, fold, fill, and crank only lends charm and frivolity to the occasion.

Matching wine and food is one of the joys of sharing a repast with companions. In pairing off a particular wine with a dish, enlist a freewheeling spirit to experiment. Set rules aren't always the last word. Red wine is making a comeback, becoming chic with shellfish or a great match for chèvre. The optimum goal is to achieve an interplay where the sum of the combination exceeds that taste pleasure of either food or wine alone. Let guests experiment, but consider their broad taste preferences in advance. Some palates lean strongly to either white or red wines.

Most important of all, entertain in a simple, yet sophisticated style. The serenity felt by the host and/or hostess extends to guests, multiplying their pleasure.

TABLE DECOR

As table decor, fresh, natural, unexpected touches often lend the greatest delight. Everyday items can provide flair at a modest tab, requiring little arranging talent or effort. Consider keynoting the table with these ideas.

• Center the table with a pot of sprouting chives or basket of tarragon for guests to snip and season their salad.

• For an aïoli supper, stripe the table with a garlic braid or wreath and tuck in yellow marguerites at random. For a Mexican brunch, utilize a red chili pepper arrangement instead.

• Let the charm of a fancifully shaped bread become an edible centerpiece. A crusty cluster of French rolls formed like a sheaf of wheat or a free-form turtle, crab, or basket are available from commercial bakers.

• Greet spring with a basket of blooming and bearing strawberries tucked in a wicker basket.

• Fill a hand-hammered copper bowl with red and green peppers, lemons, and grape leaves for an Aegean supper.

• Imbed fruits and vegetables in a wire pyramid, utilizing lemons, radishes, artichokes, and red onions, then surround with squatty yellow candles.

• Utilize straight-sided glass bowls in varying sizes to display artistic arrangements of single vegetables or fruits. One eye-catcher mates red Swiss chard in a tall cylindrical vase, nestles several red peppers and halved kiwi in a wide flat bowl, and encases a parsley bunch in a petite container. Another table adornment pairs a cylinder filled with long-stemmed strawberries with a squatty bowl bearing a large red apple immersed in water. Or magnify a cylinder of limes or lemons by pouring water in to the halfway mark.

• Line up a string of coke bottles to stand in for vases, and fill each with a purple iris or any blossom in a single color theme.

• Fill a polished wooden fruit bowl with red pomegranates, tangerines, lemons, and sprigs of cedar or mistletoe at holiday time.

• Intermix courses with a variety of china, wood, or metal utensils. Complementary textures and accents provide an interesting ambience.

BREAKFASTS
& BRUNCHES

A late-morning breakfast party on a weekend or holiday captures the fancy of many hosts and hostesses. Prized for its informality and relaxed ambience, it offers a flexible and comparatively inexpensive way to entertain any number of friends. The meal lends itself to spontaneity. The guest tally can be imprecise, since brunch fare expands or contracts with ease.

Ethnic menus automatically lend charm to the occasion. Besides, they are easy, perhaps more so than the familiar bacon-and-egg routine.

For these worldly morning spreads, the cooking may either be done on the spot, as exemplified by the fill-your-own Dutch oven omelets, roll-your-own French omelets, and fold-your-own Oriental pancakes, or the fare may be assembled completely in advance in the style of the French, Italian, and Mexican party brunches.

SERVES FOUR PERSONS

Dutch Babie
Whipped Honey Butter
Strawberries and Blueberries
Yogurt, Sour Cream, and Raw Sugar
Sliced Ham and Gouda Cheese Board
Coffee

A jaunty puffy oven omelet is a joyous way to greet breakfast guests. Besides, it goes together in a jiffy. A choice of toppings—berries, yogurt, sour cream, fluffy honey butter—lends charm. A Dutch-style meat-and-cheese board completes the repast.

SHOPPING LIST Purchase the ingredients for the special recipes, including strawberries, yogurt, sour cream, raw sugar as accompaniments for the omelet, plus thinly sliced baked ham and a round of Gouda cheese.

COOK AHEAD None is required as this breakfast takes about ten minutes to assemble.

SERVING LOGISTICS Present the pancake high and puffy at the table, then cut and let guests embellish their own serving.

DUTCH BABIE

2 tablespoons butter
4 eggs
1 cup milk
1 cup all-purpose flour
1 teaspoon freshly grated lemon peel, or 1/8 teaspoon ground nutmeg
Accompaniments: strawberries, blueberries, sour cream, yogurt, raw sugar, and Whipped Honey Butter (following)

Place butter in a 10-inch round baking pan and heat in a 425° F. oven until melted, about 5 minutes. Meanwhile, place in a blender container or food processor the eggs, milk, flour, and lemon peel or nutmeg and blend until smooth. Pour batter into the hot pan and bake in a 425° F. oven for 20 to 25 minutes, or until puffed and golden brown. Cut in wedges and serve topped with berries, sour cream, yogurt, raw sugar, or Whipped Honey Butter. Makes 4 servings.

WHIPPED HONEY BUTTER

6 tablespoons unsalted (sweet) butter, at room temperature
6 tablespoons honey

Beat butter until creamy. Add honey and beat until thick and light and fluffy. Makes about 1-1/4 cups.

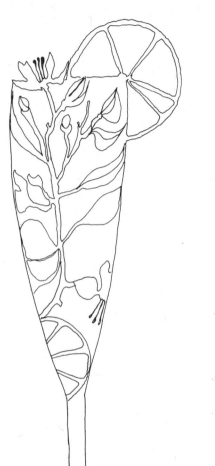

Oranges in Champagne
Gruyère Oven Omelet
Croissants and Brioche
Sweet Butter
Raspberry Jam   *Orange Marmalade*   *Peach Preserves*
Champagne
Café au Lait

Toast the morning with champagne and finish off the bottle with a splash in the fruit course. Accompany the easy oven omelet with hot croissants and brioche, easily purchased at a bakery or frozen. Have ready a pot of strong hot coffee and steaming hot milk for fusing together to compose the café au lait.

SHOPPING LIST Purchase the ingredients for the special recipes, plus the rolls and a selection of jams and jellies.

COOK AHEAD Prepare the fruit course a day in advance, but pour over the champagne at the last minute. Assemble the cheese-streaked omelet at the last minute, or arrange it in its baking dish and refrigerate overnight.

SERVING LOGISTICS Commence with champagne served in chilled glasses in the living room or the garden. Follow with the fruit course at the table and then the main course featuring the oven omelet and hot rolls.

ORANGES IN CHAMPAGNE

6 navel oranges
1-1/3 cups water
1/2 cup plus 1 tablespoon
    sugar
1/2 cup blueberries or mint
    sprigs (optional)
1/2 bottle champagne, chilled

With a vegetable peeler remove the orange part of the peel only (none of the white membrane) from 3 of the oranges. Cut the peel into fine julienne pieces. In a saucepan bring 1 cup of the water to a boil. Add orange peel and boil over medium-high heat for 5 minutes. Drain and rinse peel in cold water. In a small saucepan place 1/2 cup sugar, remaining 1/3 cup water, and the orange peel. Bring to boil, stirring, and boil gently for 5 minutes. Remove peel with a slotted spoon and let drain on paper toweling. When peel is cool, toss with the remaining tablespoon of sugar. Set aside syrup.

Peel the remaining 3 oranges, then remove the white membrane from all 6 oranges with a sharp knife. Slice oranges thinly and arrange on a serving platter or in 6 individual bowls or wine goblets. Spoon 1 tablespoon of reserved sugar syrup over each serving and chill. At serving time, pour champagne over the orange slices. Garnish with some of the candied orange peel and, if desired, a few blueberries or mint sprigs. Makes 6 servings.

NOTE Store any remaining candied peel in a tightly closed jar at room temperature. Use on other occasions when preparing this dessert, or to flavor tortes or breads.

GRUYERE OVEN OMELET

8 eggs
1 cup milk
1/2 teaspoon salt
1/4 teaspoon white pepper
1/8 teaspoon ground nutmeg
1/2 cup julienne-cut cooked
    ham
10 ounces Gruyère, samsoe,
    or Jarlsberg cheese,
    shredded (2-1/2 cups)
1 tablespoon butter, melted

Beat eggs until light and mix in milk, salt, pepper, nutmeg, ham, and cheese. Pour into a buttered 2-quart baking dish about 10-1/2 inches in diameter. Drizzle top with melted butter. Bake in a 350° F. oven for 35 minutes or until set. Makes 6 servings.

Wine Country Breakfast

Omelets
Assorted Condiments
Hot Buttered French Bread
Papaya or Melon with Lime Wedges
Coffee

Fill-Your-Own-Omelet Party

This menu works admirably for a brunch or late supper at a beach house or mountain cabin. The cook can produce a batterie of omelets in short order. Guests choose their own fillings from a choice of eight condiments.

SHOPPING LIST This is a flexible party that suits any number of guests. Allow 2 extra-large eggs per person. For eight guests figure on 1 pound thinly sliced baked ham or turkey, cut in julienne pieces; 3 avocados; 8 ounces Monterey jack or Jarlsberg cheese; 1/2 pint sour cream; 1 carton (4 ounces) alfalfa sprouts; 1 can (7 ounces) roasted sunflower seeds; 1 bottle chutney; and 1 can (4 ounces) chopped green chilies. Purchase 1 loaf French bread or 2 baguettes, sweet butter and 2 limes, and allow half of a papaya or a quarter of a cantaloupe per person.

COOK AHEAD None is required.

SERVING LOGISTICS Set up the party in the kitchen with the omelet condiments arranged in bowls within easy reach of the omelet pan. Plan to make at least two one-egg omelets per person, so guests have the option of sampling different fillings. Slice and butter the bread, wrap in foil, and heat it in a 375° F. oven ten minutes. Serve it in a basket alongside. Set out papaya halves or melon wedges on a tray, accompanied with lime wedges.

OMELETS

1 extra-large egg
1/2 teaspoon butter

Beat egg just until blended. Heat a 7- or 8-inch omelet pan, add butter, and when it stops foaming, pour in egg all at once. Slip a thin spatula under the edge of the egg just as soon as it sets and lift to let uncooked portion flow underneath. When set, but still creamy, fill with choice of filling and turn out of pan. Makes 1 serving.

This impromptu Chinese brunch goes together in a flourish with a roast chicken or turkey on hand. Arrange the Oriental vegetables in a Chinese wicker basket to delight the eye as the center-piece and then savor with dipping sauces. Dessert features fresh fruit from the market.

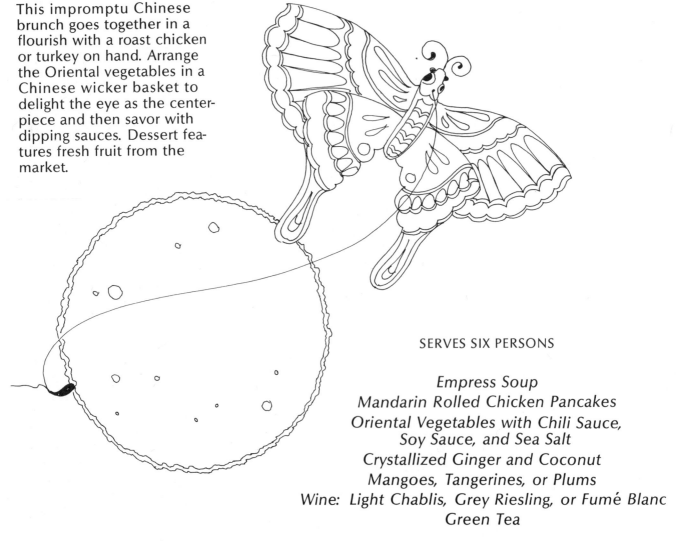

SERVES SIX PERSONS

Empress Soup
Mandarin Rolled Chicken Pancakes
Oriental Vegetables with Chili Sauce,
Soy Sauce, and Sea Salt
Crystallized Ginger and Coconut
Mangoes, Tangerines, or Plums
Wine: Light Chablis, Grey Riesling, or Fumé Blanc
Green Tea

Chinese Pancake Brunch

SHOPPING LIST   Pick up the hoisin sauce, chili sauce, and crystallized ginger and coconut at an Oriental market. Purchase the other ingredients for the special recipes. The chicken may come from a rotisserie.

COOK AHEAD None is required.

SERVING LOGISTICS This is a cooperative menu where each guest rolls his or her own pancake at the table.

EMPRESS SOUP

4 cups chicken stock
2 teaspoons soy sauce
1 teaspoon Oriental sesame oil
2 thin slices ginger root, peeled
2 green onions, cut in 1-inch lengths and the ends snipped to resemble fans
1/4 cup shelled green peas
1/2 cup shredded cooked ham, pork, or duck

Bring stock to a boil and stir in soy, sesame oil, and ginger. Simmer 5 minutes. Add onions, peas, and ham, pork, or duck and heat until hot through. Serve in small soup bowls. Makes 6 servings.

MANDARIN ROLLED CHICKEN PANCAKES

12 small flour tortillas (6-inch size)
1-1/2 tablespoons butter
4 cups slivered cooked chicken or turkey
1-1/2 tablespoons soy sauce
1 bunch (6) green onions, chopped
1 bunch cilantro, stems removed
1/4 cup toasted sesame seeds
Hoisin sauce

Place tortillas, two at a time, in a hot ungreased skillet. Heat for 30 seconds, turn over, and heat for 30 seconds longer. Then remove from pan and keep warm in a towel or wrap in aluminum foil and place in a 250° F. oven until ready to serve.

In a large skillet melt butter and sauté chicken or turkey with soy sauce just until hot. Place hot chicken or turkey, onions, cilantro, sesame seeds, and hoisin sauce in separate dishes. Let guests fill and roll their own pancakes at the table. Makes 6 servings.

ORIENTAL VEGETABLES WITH CHILI SAUCE, SOY SAUCE, AND SEA SALT

Arrange in a wicker basket sliced jícama, cut in strips; pea pods; daikon, cut in strips; Chinese cabbage, shredded; and other seasonal crisp vegetables. Serve with bowls of Chinese chili-pepper sauce, soy sauce, and sea salt.

Mexican Sangría Brunch

SERVES EIGHT PERSONS

Nachos
Chili-Jack Oven Omelet
Layered Guacamole Dip
Hot Buttered Tortillas
Pineapple Spears and Watermelon
or Honeydew Wedges
Sangría

For a summer brunch in the garden or a late Sunday-afternoon party, this colorful menu for eight adapts readily to any number of guests. The spread is decorative. Tortilla chips encircle spicy meat and beans like a sunburst. Color-packed avocado dip, scarlet Sangría, and bright fruits spark the fiesta mood.

SHOPPING LIST In addition to the ingredients for the special recipes, buy 2 dozen flour tortillas. For fruit, count on 1 pineapple and half of a watermelon or a whole honeydew melon.

COOK AHEAD Both the Nachos and the Chili-Jack Oven Omelet can be assembled a day in advance, ready for baking. The Guacamole is best made just a few hours ahead of time. The Sangría is easy to assemble just before serving.

SERVING LOGISTICS Set up the menu buffet style, either in the garden, informally in the kitchen, or in the dining room.

NACHOS

2 large onions, chopped
1 tablespoon vegetable oil
1 pound ground turkey
1 pound ground lean beef or pork
1 teaspoon salt
1/2 teaspoon ground cumin
1/2 teaspoon crumbled dried oregano
1/2 teaspoon seasoned pepper
2 garlic cloves, minced
1 can (8 ounces) tomato sauce
2 tablespoons red-wine vinegar
1 can (1 pound) refried beans
2 canned green chili peppers, seeded and chopped
10 ounces shredded Monterey jack or Cheddar cheese, shredded (2-1/2 cups)
1/4 cup commercial green taco sauce
1 cup sour cream
2/3 cup pitted ripe olives
6 small pickled sweet red peppers

Cilantro sprigs
1 package (15 ounces) tortilla chips

Using a large frying pan sauté onions in oil until golden brown. Add ground meats and cook, stirring, until browned. Season with salt, cumin, oregano, seasoned pepper, and garlic. Stir in tomato sauce and vinegar, cover, and simmer 30 minutes, stirring occasionally.

Spread beans in a large shallow baking pan or oven-proof platter, about 11 inches in diameter. Spoon over meat sauce. Scatter over chili peppers. Sprinkle with cheese and dot with taco sauce. Cover and chill, if making ahead. Bake uncovered in a 400° F. oven for 25 to 30 minutes or until heated through. Remove from the oven and spread sour cream over the center. Garnish with olives, pickled peppers, and cilantro sprigs. Tuck tortilla chips around the edge. Makes 8 servings.

LAYERED GUACAMOLE DIP

Guacamole (following)
1 cup sour cream
1/2 teaspoon ground cumin
1/2 teaspoon chili powder
3 green onions, chopped
1 large tomato, peeled and
  chopped
3 ounces Monterey jack
  cheese, shredded (3/4 cup)
3/4 cup sliced ripe olives
Tortilla chips

Prepare the Guacamole. Mix together sour cream, cumin, and chili powder and spread on an 8-inch plate with a rimmed edge. Cover with Guacamole, making an even layer. Sprinkle the green onions in the center and encircle with rings of tomato, cheese, and olives. Poke tortilla chips around the edge and serve additional chips in a basket. Makes 8 servings.

GUACAMOLE Halve 2 avocados, remove pits, reserving them, and scoop pulp into a bowl. Mash with a fork and mix in 1/4 cup fresh lemon juice, 3 tablespoons each chopped onions and cilantro, 1/4 teaspoon salt, and dash of Tabasco sauce. If made ahead, poke pits into Guacamole to prevent it from darkening.

CHILI–JACK OVEN OMELET

6 eggs
3/4 cup milk
1/4 teaspoon salt
1/4 cup diced canned green
  chili peppers
1/4 teaspoon ground cumin
1/4 teaspoon crumbled dried
  oregano
1/4 teaspoon garlic salt
1/4 teaspoon seasoned pepper
8 ounces Monterey jack
  cheese, shredded (2 cups)

Beat eggs until light and mix in milk, salt, chili peppers, cumin, oregano, garlic salt, seasoned pepper, and cheese. Turn into a lightly buttered 9-inch pie pan. Bake in a 350° F. oven for 35 minutes, or until puffed and golden. Cut in wedges to serve. Makes 8 servings.

SANGRIA

3 liters zinfandel or Burgundy
  wine, chilled
3 cups orange juice, chilled
2/3 cup fresh lemon juice,
  chilled
1/3 cup sugar
1/4 cup brandy
1/4 cup Cointreau or other
  orange-flavored liqueur
1 bottle (23 ounces) mineral
  water, chilled
Ice
2 oranges, very thinly sliced
2 lemons, very thinly sliced

Pour chilled wine, orange juice, and lemon juice into a large punch bowl. Add sugar, brandy, and Cointreau and stir to blend. Pour in mineral water and add ice. Float orange and lemon slices on top at the last minute. Makes about 5 quarts, ample for 8 servings.

Tuscany Breakfast

Melon or Winter Pears with Prosciutto
Panettone Milano
Galliano Whipped Cream Cheese
Amaretti (optional)
Cappuccino

This north Italian brunch suits all seasons. Serve whichever suggested fruit is at its prime along with prosciutto for a first course. If desired, buy the fruit-filled panettone at your favorite Italian bakery. An espresso pot with milk steamer is essential to achieve a true cappuccino, a blend of equal parts espresso and frothy steamed milk.

SHOPPING LIST Purchase the ingredients for the special recipes. If desired, have some amaretti (Italian almond macaroons) on hand for extra munching.

COOK AHEAD Bake the bread in advance and freeze it, if desired. Let thaw and reheat to serve. Make the Galliano Whipped Cream Cheese a day ahead. Assemble the fruit and prosciutto just before serving.

SERVING LOGISTICS Present the meal at the table.

MELON OR WINTER PEARS WITH PROSCIUTTO

1 large cantaloupe or crenshaw
    melon, or 4 comice or
    anjou pears
24 wafer-thin slices prosciutto
Freshly ground black pepper

Halve melon, scoop out seeds, peel, and cut into 24 crescent slices. Wrap each slice with a slice of prosciutto and arrange four slices on a plate for each serving. Or peel pears, halve, core, and cut each half into thirds. Wrap each pear slice with a slice of prosciutto. Grind on a light dusting of pepper or pass the grinder at the table.

PANETTONE MILANO

1 package (1 tablespoon)
    active dry yeast
1/4 cup lukewarm water
3/4 cup milk
1/4 pound (1/2 cup) butter,
    at room temperature
1/3 cup sugar
3 eggs
3-1/2 cups all-purpose flour
1 teaspoon vanilla extract
1 teaspoon freshly grated
    lemon peel
1 teaspoon salt
1/4 teaspoon ground nutmeg
1/2 cup golden raisins
1/2 cup pine nuts or slivered
    blanched almonds
Almond Paste Topping
    (following)

Sprinkle yeast into lukewarm water, stir to dissolve, and let stand until foamy, about 10 minutes. Heat milk to lukewarm. In a large mixing bowl beat butter and sugar until creamy. Add eggs, one at a time, and beat until smooth. Add 1 cup of the flour and beat well. Mix in yeast, luke-warm milk, vanilla extract, lemon peel, salt, and nutmeg. Gradually add remaining 2-1/2 cups flour, beating until smooth. Mix in raisins and nuts. Turn out on a lightly floured board and knead until smooth and no longer sticky. Place in a bowl, cover with a clean kitchen towel, and let rise in a warm place for about 1-1/2 hours, or until doubled in bulk.

Punch down dough, turn out on a lightly floured board, and knead lightly. Divide in half. Shape into 2 rounds each about 7 inches in diam-eter, and place each on a greased baking sheet. Cover and let rise in a warm place until doubled in size, about 45 minutes. Spread with Almond Paste Topping. Bake in a 325° F. oven for 35 or 40 minutes, or until the loaves sound hollow when thumped. Remove to a wire rack to cool. Serve warm or at room tem-perature, sliced and accom-panied with sweet butter and Galliano Whipped Cream Cheese. Makes two 7-inch round loaves.

ALMOND PASTE TOPPING Beat together 1 egg white, 6 table-spoons almond paste, and 2 tablespoons sugar until smooth.

GALLIANO WHIPPED CREAM CHEESE

8 ounces natural cream
   cheese, at room temperature
2 tablespoons sugar
1-1/2 tablespoons Galliano
   or amaretto liqueur or rum
2 tablespoons whipping cream

Place in a mixing bowl or a food processor the cheese, sugar, liqueur of choice or rum, and cream. Beat until blended. Mound on a serving plate or small footed compote and swirl into a cone shape. Chill until serving time. Makes 6 servings.

LUNCHES
& PICNICS

Midday parties fill a definite entertaining role. More relaxed than a dinner, they are a perfect way to cherish special moments with close friends. Count them ideal for a wide variety of occasions, from a large-scale charity gathering to a family celebration or a wine-country picnic.

The informality and simplicity of luncheon parties deems them less taxing for the host or hostess. The menu is often briefer than for dinner, making cooking chores less ambitious.

A very pleasant aspect of a luncheon is that it suits most any setting: the garden, poolside deck, kitchen, dining room, or sunny meadow or beachfront site.

A light, refreshing aperitif or wine enhances the ambience. Or today, where a casual style of entertaining predominates, guests may even opt for chilled mineral water or a tall, cool beer.

SERVES SIX PERSONS

Gougère with Gruyère Nuggets
Hot Sausage and Romaine Salad
Brie and Baguette
Strawberries in Wine
Wine: Pinot Noir or Gamay Beaujolais
Coffee

Sunday Bistro Lunch

This charming French luncheon is perfect for an informal weekend gathering either at home, or with house guests at a weekend cabin. The menu goes together with ease. A cheese-studded bread ring, sausage-embellished salad, and berries in wine star. Why not enlist a guest to help hull the berries or dice the cheese?

SHOPPING HINTS Purchase the ingredients for the special recipes, plus a wedge of brie, a baguette, and sweet butter.

COOK AHEAD None is required.

SERVING LOGISTICS Present the gougère hot from the oven along with the salad. Follow with a cheese course, and then the berries steeped in wine.

GOUGERE WITH GRUYERE NUGGETS

3/4 cup milk
3/4 cup water
1/2 teaspoon salt
1/4 pound (1/2 cup) butter
1-1/2 cups all-purpose flour
5 eggs
8 ounces Gruyère cheese, diced (2 cups)

Butter and flour a 12-inch pizza pan or large baking sheet; set aside. Using a large saucepan heat to boiling the milk, water, salt, and butter. Remove from heat, add flour all at once, and beat with a wooden spoon until it clings together in a ball. Transfer to a mixing bowl. Add eggs, one at a time, beating after each one until smooth. Reserve 1/2 cup cheese for topping and mix remainder into the dough. Spoon out into a wreath shape on the prepared baking pan. Top with reserved cheese. Bake in a 400° F. oven for 30 to 35 minutes, or until golden brown. Makes 6 servings.

HOT SAUSAGE
AND ROMAINE SALAD

3 mild Italian sausages
2 slices French bread, cubed
1 tablespoon butter
1 garlic clove, minced
1 head Romaine lettuce
3 slices bacon, diced
1/4 cup olive oil
2 tablespoons red-wine
   vinegar
1/4 teaspoon salt
1/4 teaspoon freshly ground
   black pepper
1 teaspoon Dijon-style
   mustard
8 cherry tomatoes, halved

Place sausages in a saucepan, add water to cover, cover pan, and bring to a boil. Remove from heat and let stand 15 minutes. In a small frying pan sauté bread cubes in butter until golden; add garlic and toss to mix well; set aside. Tear Romaine into bite-size pieces and place in a large salad bowl. Cook bacon until crisp. Remove with slotted spoon and drain on paper toweling; reserve drippings. Shake together oil, vinegar, salt, pepper, and mustard. Pour over greens. Add 3 table-spoons of the hot reserved bacon drippings and mix lightly. Drain sausage and slice thinly. Scatter sausage slices, bacon, and tomatoes over greens. Makes 6 servings.

STRAWBERRIES IN RED WINE

1 quart strawberries, hulled
1/3 cup sugar (or more, if
   desired)
About 2 cups dry fruity red
   wine, such as zinfandel or
   gamay beaujolais

Alternate berries and sugar in a tall wide-mouthed cylindrical jar or glass serving container. Pour over enough wine to cover. Let stand at room tem-perature for 3 to 4 hours before serving. Makes 6 servings.

Turkish Sunday Lunch

SERVES EIGHT PERSONS

Honeydew and Crenshaw with Salami
Cheese Boerek
Mushroom and Veal Boerek
Sliced Tomatoes and Cucumbers with Herbs
Frozen Yogurt and Berry Sundaes
Wine: California Gewürztraminer,
Alsatian Riesling, or White Zinfandel

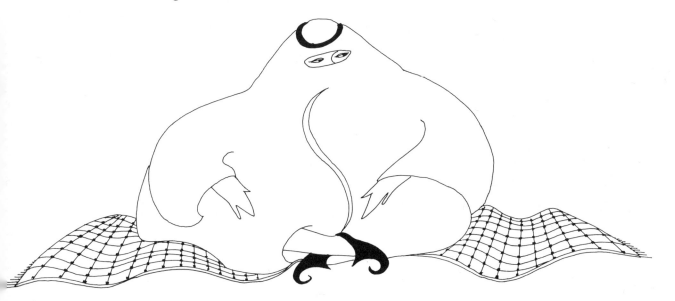

Two kinds of flaky boereks, made in advance, star at this noon-time party meal. Melon with salami makes a swift, refreshing first course. Frozen yogurt embellished with berries and pistachios is an apropos finale.

SHOPPING LIST Purchase the ingredients for the special recipes.

COOK AHEAD Assemble the boereks a day in advance and refrigerate, if desired. Or make well in advance but do not bake them, wrap well, and freeze for two or three weeks. Let thaw before baking. A few hours ahead of time arrange the melon with salami and slice the tomatoes and cucumbers. For an easy presentation later, scoop the yogurt into small balls and refreeze, ready for instant serving.

SERVING LOGISTICS Serve the menu buffet style or at the table in three courses.

HONEYDEW AND CRENSHAW WITH SALAMI

1 honeydew melon
1 crenshaw melon, or
  2 cantaloupes
16 slices salami
Freshly ground black pepper

Halve honeydew and crenshaw or cantaloupes, scoop out seeds, and peel. Cut honeydew and crenshaw into 8 wedges or each cantaloupe into quarters. On each of 8 plates arrange 2 honeydew and 2 crenshaw or cantaloupe wedges, alternating colors. Drape each serving with 2 pieces of salami. Grind pepper over the top. Makes 8 servings.

CHEESE BOEREK

1 package (10 ounces) frozen
  puff pastry shells (6 shells)
4 ounces Swiss or Gruyère
  cheese
4 ounces cream cheese
4 ounces feta cheese
8 ounces (1 cup) small-curd
  or large-curd cottage cheese
2 egg yolks
1/4 cup parsley sprigs
1/4 cup chopped chives or
  green onions
1/4 teaspoon salt
1/4 teaspoon freshly ground
  black pepper
1 tablespoon butter, melted

Lay out pastry shells on a board, cover with plastic wrap, and let warm to room temperature. Using a food processor fitted with a steel blade, shred the Swiss or Gruyère cheese and turn into a mixing bowl. (Or grate the cheese by hand.) Place in the container of the food processor (or a blender) the cream cheese, feta cheese, cottage cheese, egg yolks, parsley, chives or green onions, salt, and pepper. Process just until smoothly blended. Turn into the bowl with the shredded cheese and mix lightly.

Stack 3 pastry shells on a lightly floured board and roll out into a 14-inch round. Place dough round on a 12-inch pizza pan with edges overlapping. Spread with cheese filling. Stack remaining 3 pastry shells and roll out into a 14-inch round. Place round on top of filling, brush overlapping edges of dough with water, and press to seal edges of pastry rounds. Turn back pastry edges and crimp edges. Chill thoroughly, at least 30 minutes, or freeze for 10 minutes for pastry to firm up. (If desired, the boerek may be wrapped and frozen at this point. Thaw before baking.)

To bake, brush top with melted butter and bake in a 425° F. oven for 20 to 25 minutes, or until puffed and golden brown. Cut into wedges to serve. Makes 8 servings.

MUSHROOM AND VEAL BOEREK

1 package (10 ounces) frozen puff pastry shells (6)
1 tablespoon plus 1 teaspoon butter
1 large onion, finely chopped
1/4 pound mushrooms, chopped
1 pound ground veal, beef, or turkey
3/4 teaspoon salt
1/2 teaspoon crumbled dried tarragon
1/4 teaspoon freshly ground black pepper
2 tablespoons chopped parsley
2 garlic cloves, minced
1/2 cup shredded Parmesan or Romano cheese
1 tablespoon butter, melted

Thaw pastry shells as directed for Cheese Boerek, preceding. To make the filling, melt 1 tablespoon butter in a large skillet and sauté onion until glazed. Add the mushrooms and sauté 1 minute; turn out of pan into mixing bowl. Melt 1 teaspoon butter in the same skillet, add veal, beef, or turkey, and cook, stirring, until meat loses its pink color. Season with salt, tarragon, pepper, parsley, and garlic, remove from the heat, and turn into the bowl with the sautéed onion. Mix in the Parmesan or Romano cheese and let cool. Prepare the pastry as directed for Cheese Boerek, preceding, filling with mushroom-veal mixture, and proceed as directed, brushing the top with melted butter before baking. Makes 8 servings.

TOMATOES AND CUCUMBERS WITH HERBS

6 large tomatoes, peeled
    and sliced
2 large cucumbers, peeled
    and sliced
Romaine lettuce leaves
Salt and freshly ground black
    pepper
2 tablespoons chopped fresh
    basil or chives

Arrange tomato and cucumber slices on a large platter lined with Romaine leaves. Season with salt and pepper and sprinkle with basil or chives. Cover with plastic wrap and chill until serving time. Makes 8 servings.

FROZEN YOGURT AND BERRY SUNDAES

1 quart lemon-flavored frozen
    yogurt
1 quart raspberry-flavored
    frozen yogurt
1 quart strawberries, hulled
1/2 cup finely chopped
    pistachios or toasted
    slivered blanched almonds
Pitcher of Grand Marnier
    (optional)

Scoop yogurt into small balls, forming 8 scoops of each flavor, and refreeze. To serve, set out bowls of yogurt balls and accompany with bowls of strawberries and nuts and a pitcher of Grand Marnier. Let guests assemble their own desserts. Makes 8 servings.

All-Seasons' Continental Picnic

SERVES SIX PERSONS

Carrot-Cashew Soup
Stuffed Veal Rolls
Mushroom and Red Pepper Garnish
Apples in a Basket
Rum Raisin Brownies
Wine: Chardonnay,
Tavel Rosé, or Alsatian or California Sylvaner

This enticing, quite glamorous luncheon is ideal for an outdoor picnic any time of the year. On a brisk day, serve the creamy carrot soup hot from a thermos. On a balmy day, offer it chilled. The veal rolls, which can be sliced so the pretty pinwheels of stuffing are revealed, are good at room temperature or chilled. Finish off with fruit savored out of hand and rum-laced brownies.

SHOPPING LIST Purchase the ingredients for the special recipes, plus a half-dozen apples.

COOK AHEAD Prepare the entire meal a day in advance, if desired. Refrigerate the soup and meat; store the brownies in a can.

SERVING LOGISTICS A tailgate or a table in a park will accommodate the picnic menu. Pack the luncheon with ease in a basket and tote along a gay vinyl tablecloth.

CARROT–CASHEW SOUP

6 large carrots, peeled and cut in 1-inch lengths
2 large onions, quartered
2 garlic cloves
1 turnip, peeled and quartered
4 cups chicken stock
1/2 teaspoon salt
1/2 teaspoon freshly ground black pepper
1/2 teaspoon ground allspice
1/4 cup chopped roasted cashews or whole sunflower seeds or pistachios

Place in a large saucepot the carrots, onions, garlic cloves, turnip, chicken stock, salt, pepper, and allspice. Cover and simmer for 15 to 20 minutes, or until the vegetables are fork tender. Let cool slightly and purée in a blender or food processor. If a thinner soup is desired, add more stock. Serve hot or cold, garnished with roasted nuts or seeds. Makes 6 servings.

STUFFED VEAL ROLLS

6 veal cutlets, or 1-1/4 pounds tender beef, such as sirloin tip, thinly sliced
Salt and freshly ground black pepper for seasoning meat
1 large onion, chopped
2 tablespoons butter
3/4 pound ground veal or turkey
1 garlic clove, minced
1/4 cup minced parsley
1/2 cup plus 3 tablespoons dry sherry or dry vermouth
1/2 teaspoon salt
1/2 teaspoon freshly ground black pepper
1/2 teaspoon crumbled dried thyme
6 slices boiled ham

Pound veal or beef to 1/8-inch thickness. Sprinkle lightly with salt and pepper. Sauté onion in 1 tablespoon of the butter in a medium skillet, cooking until glazed. Mix together ground veal or turkey, garlic, sautéed onion, parsley, 3 tablespoons sherry or vermouth, salt, pepper, and thyme. Cover each slice of veal or beef with a ham slice, then cover with a thin layer of the ground meat filling. Roll up in a cylinder shape and tie with string. Heat remaining 1 tablespoon butter in a large skillet. Add rolls and cook, turning to brown all sides. Add 1/2 cup sherry or vermouth. Cover and simmer for 10 minutes, or until just tender. Remove rolls from skillet and let cool. Serve cold or at room temperature, thinly sliced if desired. Makes 6 servings.

MUSHROOM AND RED PEPPER GARNISH

Ring the platter of meat rolls with button mushrooms tossed in chopped parsley and a few pickled sweet red peppers or cherry tomatoes.

RUM RAISIN BROWNIES

1/2 cup golden or dark raisins
1/4 cup dark rum
1/4 pound (1/2 cup) butter
4 ounces unsweetened
    chocolate
1 ounce semisweet chocolate
3 eggs
1-1/4 cups sugar
1 teaspoon vanilla extract
1 cup all-purpose flour
1/4 teaspoon salt
1/2 cup coarsely chopped
    walnuts or pecans

Soak raisins in rum for 20 minutes. Combine butter and chocolates in the top pan of a double boiler and melt over hot water; stir to blend, then cool slightly. Beat eggs until thick and lemon-colored and gradually beat in sugar. Stir in chocolate-butter mixture, vanilla extract, flour, and salt, mixing just until blended. Mix in nuts, raisins, and rum. Pour into a buttered and floured 9-inch square pan. Bake in a 350° F. oven for 25 minutes, or until set but still moist. Let cool, then cut into squares. Makes about 24.

SERVES FOUR PERSONS

Tossed Shredded Chicken Salad
Soy Crackers
Tropical Fruit Ices
Mineral Water with Lime
Green Tea

This refreshing salad luncheon is readily assembled with a preroasted broiler chicken. Prepare an extra one when roasting chicken for dinner or purchase one from a rotisserie. Enhance the meal with lively soy crackers for nibblers and finish off with exotic tropical ices.

SHOPPING LIST Go to an Oriental market for a selection of two or three kinds of soy or sesame crackers for the salad accompaniment. Purchase the ingredients for the special recipes, including a trio of contrasting-colored fruit ices from an ice cream store or the freezer section of a supermarket.

COOK AHEAD Assemble the salad ingredients and dressing a day in advance. Wait to shred lettuce and toss just before serving.

SERVING LOGISTICS Serve the salad luncheon plates at the table with dessert to follow.

TOSSED SHREDDED CHICKEN SALAD

2-1/2- to 3-pound roasted broiler chicken, or 4 cooked split chicken breasts
Sesame-Soy Dressing (following)
2 cups shredded iceberg lettuce or Napa cabbage
1 bunch cilantro, stems removed
1/3 cup slivered jícama or water chestnuts
2 green onions, cut in 1/2-inch lengths and the ends snipped to resemble fans
3 tablespoons toasted sesame seeds
1/3 cup toasted slivered blanched almonds
1 kiwi fruit, peeled and sliced, or 1/3 pound seedless green grapes in 4 small bunches
4 large strawberries

Skin and bone broiler chicken or chicken breasts and tear or cut meat into strips. Cover and chill. Prepare Sesame-Soy Dressing. At serving time, place chicken strips in a bowl, pour over half of the Sesame-Soy Dressing, and mix well. Add lettuce, cilantro, jícama or water chestnuts, onions, sesame seeds, and almonds. Add remaining dressing and mix lightly. Divide evenly among 4 Oriental soup bowls or plates. Garnish each plate with a slice of kiwi or a bunch of grapes and a strawberry. Makes 4 servings.

SESAME-SOY DRESSING In a small bowl combine 1/2 teaspoon *each* dry mustard and freshly grated lemon peel, 2 tablespoons *each* honey, soy sauce, Oriental sesame oil, and fresh lemon juice, and 1/4 cup safflower oil.

TROPICAL FRUIT ICES

1/2 pint *each* of three fruit ices: pineapple, mango, kiwi, lemon, lime, or raspberry
Blossoms: nasturtiums, fuschias, or cyclamen

Scoop ices into balls and arrange a small scoop of each of 3 flavors in 4 dessert bowls or large-bowled wine goblets. Garnish each with a blossom. Makes 4 servings.

Oriental Chicken Salad Lunch

Fast Portable Croissant Picnic

SERVES FOUR PERSONS

Croissant Sandwiches
Marinated Mushroom Salad
Pears and Grapes
Choice Butter Cookies
Wine: Grenache Rosé or Blanc de Noir

For a spur-of-the-moment occasion, this menu goes together with little effort. Flaky croissants are the backbone of delicious sandwiches to partner with a tantalizing salad that marinates as it totes. Fruit in season complements a premium assortment of packaged cookies for dessert.

SHOPPING HINTS Stop at a favorite bakery for the croissants or purchase frozen ones. Also pick up some butter cookies, pears, and grapes. Buy the items for the special recipes.

COOK AHEAD None is required.

SERVING LOGISTICS This menu spreads out with ease at a park or any informal setting.

CROISSANT SANDWICHES

4 croissants, split and buttered
4 ounces sliced smoked
   salmon or pastrami
4 ounces natural cream
   cheese or thinly sliced
   Muenster cheese
Chopped chives (optional)

Open the croissants and layer them either with salmon and cream cheese or pastrami and Muenster. Garnish with chives. Wrap and carry in an insulated container. Makes 4 servings.

MARINATED MUSHROOM SALAD

Tarragon Dressing (following)
3/4 pound mushrooms, thinly
   sliced
1 cup thinly sliced celery
1 basket cherry tomatoes,
   halved
4 ounces Jarlsberg or Gruyère
   cheese, shredded (1 cup)
2 tablespoons chopped
   parsley

Prepare the Tarragon Dressing. Place in a bowl the mushrooms and celery, pour over Tarragon Dressing, and mix lightly. Cover and chill for 1 or 2 hours. Or pack immediately in a wide-mouthed jar and carry in an insulated container. At serving time, top with a ring of tomatoes and scatter over the cheese. Sprinkle with parsley. Makes 4 servings.

TARRAGON DRESSING Mix together in a small container 1/4 cup olive oil, 1-1/2 tablespoons fresh lemon juice, 1/4 teaspoon *each* salt and crumbled dried tarragon, 1/8 teaspoon freshly ground black pepper, and 1/2 teaspoon *each* Dijon-style mustard and freshly grated lemon peel.

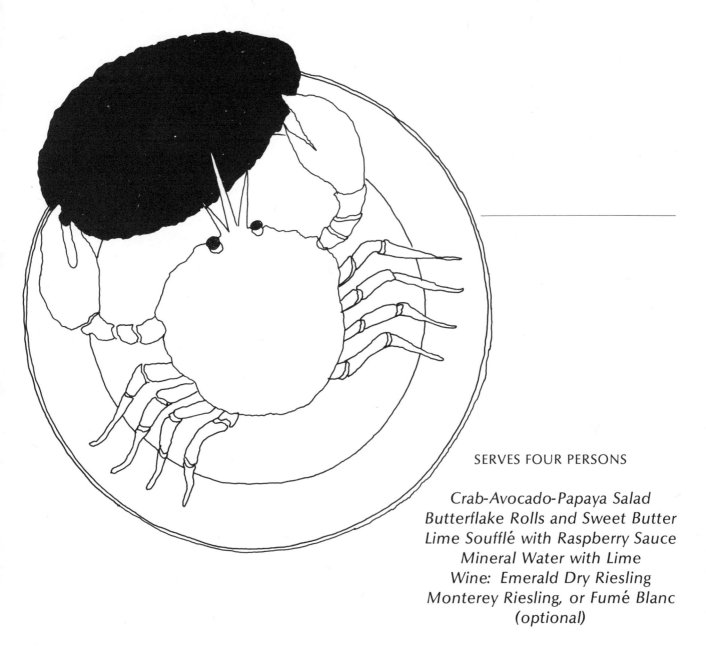

SERVES FOUR PERSONS

Crab-Avocado-Papaya Salad
Butterflake Rolls and Sweet Butter
Lime Soufflé with Raspberry Sauce
Mineral Water with Lime
Wine: Emerald Dry Riesling
Monterey Riesling, or Fumé Blanc
(optional)

Crab Season Lunch

In season, fresh Dungeness crab meat makes a regal pivot for a captivating salad luncheon. Other seafoods stand in admirably, as well: bay shrimp, cold diced lobster, or poached scallops. Finish off with a pouffy lime or lemon soufflé splashed with a purée of raspberries.

SHOPPING LIST Purchase the ingredients for the special recipes, plus the rolls and sweet butter.

COOK AHEAD Mix the salad dressing in advance and chill. The salads may be assembled a couple hours ahead and refrigerated. Assemble the ingredients for the soufflés, ready to whip up in a jiffy between courses.

SERVING LOOGISTICS Present the luncheon at the table in two courses.

CRAB–AVOCADO–PAPAYA SALAD

Lemon-Tarragon Dressing (page 42)
1 large papaya, or 2 pink grapefruit
2 medium avocados
Fresh lemon juice
Butter lettuce
3/4 pound cooked crab meat, small shrimp, or diced lobster, or poached scallops
1/4 cup toasted slivered blanched almonds, chopped macadamia nuts, or chopped pistachios

Prepare the Lemon-Tarragon Dressing. Peel and halve papaya and scoop out seeds. Slice papaya halves lengthwise. Or peel and section grapefruits. Peel and slice avocados and sprinkle slices with lemon juice to prevent darkening. Arrange a bed of butter lettuce on 4 dinner-size plates. Spoon a mound of crab meat or other seafood onto the center of each lettuce bed and surround with a pinwheel of alternating papaya slices or grapefruit sections and avocado slices. Cover and chill. To serve, spoon over Lemon-Tarragon Dressing and sprinkle with toasted nuts. Makes 4 servings.

LEMON-TARRAGON DRESSING

Combine in a small bowl or jar 1/3 cup safflower oil, 2 tablespoons fresh lemon juice, 1 tablespoon white-wine vinegar, 1/2 teaspoon *each* freshly grated lemon peel and crumbled dried tarragon, and 1/4 teaspoon *each* salt and Dijon-style mustard.

LIME SOUFFLE WITH RASPBERRY SAUCE

1-1/2 teaspoons freshly grated lime or lemon peel
1/4 cup plus 1/2 teaspoon granulated sugar
5 egg whites
1/8 teaspoon salt
1/8 teaspoon cream of tartar
3 egg yolks
3 tablespoons fresh lime or lemon juice
2 teaspoons powdered sugar
Raspberry Sauce (following)

Place lime or lemon peel in a small bowl, add 1/2 teaspoon of the granulated sugar, and mash with the back of a spoon to extract the oils; set aside. Using a large mixing bowl beat the egg whites until foamy; add the salt and cream of tartar and beat until soft peaks form. Add 2 tablespoons of the granulated sugar and beat until stiff, glossy peaks form. In another bowl beat the egg yolks until pale and lemon-colored; then beat in the remaining 2 tablespoons granulated sugar, lemon juice, and lemon peel. Fold one-third of the whites into the yolks to lighten them, then gently fold in the remaining whites. Turn into 4 buttered individual soufflé dishes. Dust tops with powdered sugar shaken through a wire strainer. Bake in a 400° F. oven for 8 to 10 minutes, or until risen and a light golden brown. Serve immediately. Slash the center of each and pour in Raspberry Sauce. Makes 4 servings.

RASPBERRY SAUCE Thaw 1 package (10 ounces) frozen raspberries. Purée in a blender or food processor, then force through a wire sieve, discarding seeds. Pour purée into a pitcher to serve.

SERVES FOUR PERSONS

Sautéed Camembert
Shrimp-stuffed Artichokes
Baguette and Sweet Butter
Sliced Oranges and Kiwis
Grand Marnier Truffles
Wine: Johannisberg Riesling or Chardonnay
Iced Tea

California Bounty Luncheon

This simple, sophisticated menu embraces the fresh bounty of the marketplace in a light, any-season spread. It totes with ease for a picnic outing if one serves the cheese at room temperature. Tender artichokes are the natural container for an herb-shrimp filling. Liqueur-imbued truffles lend a chic touch, yet are a snap to do.

SHOPPING LIST Buy the ingredients for the special recipes, plus a baguette and sweet butter.

COOK AHEAD Cook the artichokes a day ahead, if desired. Make the truffle candies up

to a week in advance and refrigerate. All of the other preparations can be done quickly.

SERVING LOGISTICS Present the menu in three courses, serving the cheese as an appetizer in the garden or living room, then the artichokes and dessert at the table.

SAUTEED CAMEMBERT

1 egg
4-ounce round camembert
  cheese, chilled
Finely crushed soda-cracker
  crumbs
3 tablespoons butter
2 tablespoons chopped chives
Thin wheat wafers

Beat egg until blended in a small bowl. Dip cheese round in egg, turning to coat both sides, then roll in cracker crumbs just to coat. Melt butter in a small skillet and sauté cheese quickly, turning to brown both sides and heating until cheese is slightly soft inside. Place on a serving plate and sprinkle with chives. Surround with crackers. Makes 4 servings.

SHRIMP–STUFFED ARTICHOKES

Yogurt-Sour Cream Chive
  Dressing (following)
4 large artichokes, cooked
  and chilled
Butter lettuce
1/2 pound cooked small
  shrimp
2 tomatoes, cut in wedges
12 pitted ripe olives

Prepare Yogurt-Sour Cream Chive Dressing. Pull out the center leaves of the artichokes and scoop out the chokes. Arrange butter lettuce leaves on individual serving plates and place an artichoke on each bed of greens. Spoon 1 tablespoon of dressing in the center of each artichoke and top with shrimp. Ring with tomato wedges and olives. Pass remaining dressing. Makes 4 servings.

YOGURT-SOUR CREAM CHIVE DRESSING Stir together in a bowl 1/3 cup *each* plain yogurt and sour cream, 1 teaspoon *each* fresh lemon juice and Dijon-style mustard, 3 table-spoons finely chopped parsley, and 1 tablespoon minced chives.

SLICED ORANGES AND KIWIS

4 oranges
2 kiwi fruit
6 large strawberries, or 1/4
  cup blueberries (optional)
2 tablespoons Grand Marnier
  or other orange-flavored
  liqueur

Peel and slice oranges thinly and arrange in a circle, over-lapping slices, on 4 dessert plates. Peel and slice kiwis and radiate slices from the center of each circle. Adorn with berries, if desired, and spoon over Grand Marnier. Makes 4 servings.

GRAND MARNIER CHOCOLATE TRUFFLES

6 ounces semisweet chocolate
2 tablespoons whipping cream
1 tablespoon Grand Marnier
2 tablespoons unsweetened
  chocolate or cocoa powder

In the top pan of a double boiler, combine chocolate, cream, and Grand Marnier and melt over hot water, stirring to blend. Refrigerate until mixture begins to firm up, about 15 to 20 minutes. Make a thin, even layer of chocolate or cocoa powder on a sheet of waxed paper. With 2 spoons shape chocolate into marble-size balls and roll in chocolate or cocoa powder to coat evenly. When balls are coated, arrange in a single layer in a waxed paper-lined tin. Cover and refrigerate. Let warm to room temperature about 15 minutes before serv-ing. Makes 18 to 20.

Stand-up Quiche Party

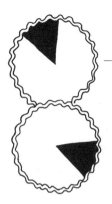

SERVES TWENTY PERSONS

Nosegay of Crudités with Green Goddess Sauce
Choice of Quiches: Chili-Jack, Mushroom and Sausage, Seafood
Chocolate-dipped Strawberries or Tangerines
Wines: Fumé Blanc, Sauvignon Blanc, Muscadet, and/or Vouvray

Certain gala occasions, such as an art gallery showing or boutique opening, call for a light repast in a walk-about situation. A selection of quiches makes an appealing spread for such a gathering. A nosegay of crudités provides a fetching centerpiece for easy dipping. Fruit sealed in chocolate lends a delectable sweet touch. This party plan is ideal for a summer garden party as well, providing ample fare for twenty guests.

SHOPPING LIST Purchase the ingredients for the special recipes.

COOK AHEAD Make the Green Goddess Sauce up to two days ahead and refrigerate. Assemble and bake the quiches a day ahead, then reheat. The fruit may be dipped the day of the party.

SERVING LOGISTICS Set up the party buffet style. Cut quiches in small wedges so guests may sample more than one kind.

NOSEGAY OF CRUDITES WITH GREEN GODDESS SAUCE

3/4 cup mayonnaise (prefer-
    ably homemade)
1/2 cup chopped parsley
3 tablespoons white-wine
    vinegar
1 garlic clove, minced
1 teaspoon chopped fresh
    tarragon, or 1/4 teaspoon
    crumbled dried tarragon
4 anchovy fillets
1/2 cup sour cream
Freshly ground black pepper
Assorted raw vegetables:
    cherry tomatoes, mush-
    rooms, pea pods, carrots,
    radishes, zucchini, cucumber,
    fennel, cauliflower
Romaine lettuce leaves
    (optional)

Place in the container of a blender or a food processor fitted with a steel blade the mayonnaise, parsley, vinegar, garlic, tarragon, and anchovy fillets. Blend or process until parsley is very finely minced. Add sour cream and blend just until incorporated. Turn into a jar, cover, and refrigerate. To serve, spoon sauce into a bowl or stoneware container. Cut vegetables into pieces suitable for dipping and assemble in a basket, using a flower frog, if you wish, to hold them in place. Tuck Romaine leaves between, if desired. Makes about 1-1/2 cups sauce.

CHILI–JACK QUICHE

Press-In Pastry (following)
4 eggs
1-1/2 cups half-and-half cream
1/4 teaspoon ground cumin
1/4 teaspoon crumbled dried
    oregano
1/2 teaspoon salt
Dash of freshly ground black
    pepper
3 tablespoons chopped canned
    green chili peppers
6 ounces Monterey jack
    cheese, shredded (1-1/2 cups)
1 tablespoon butter

Prepare Press-In Pastry. In a mixing bowl beat eggs until blended and mix in the half-and-half cream, cumin, oregano, salt, pepper, chilies, and cheese. Turn into the pastry-lined pan and dot with butter. Bake in a 425° F. oven for 10 minutes; reduce heat to 350° F. and bake 30 minutes longer, or until set. Remove pan sides and cut into wedges to serve. Makes 8 to 10 servings.

PRESS-IN PASTRY In a mixing bowl or container of a food processor fitted with a steel blade, place 1-1/4 cups all-purpose flour and 1/4 pound (1/2 cup) butter and mix until butter is crumbly. Add 1 egg yolk and 1 to 2 tablespoons ice water and mix just until distributed. Pat crumbly dough into the bottom and sides of an 11-inch flan pan with 1-inch sides and re-movable bottom. Chill until firm. Partially bake in a 400° F. oven for 8 minutes. Let cool before filling.

MUSHROOM AND SAUSAGE QUICHE

Press-In Pastry (preceding)
3 mild Italian sausages (about
    10 ounces)
1/2 pound mushrooms,
    chopped
2 green onions, chopped
3 tablespoons butter
4 eggs
1 cup half-and-half cream
1/2 teaspoon salt
1/2 teaspoon crumbled dried
    tarragon
4 ounces Gruyère or Swiss
    cheese, shredded (1 cup)

Prepare Press-In Pastry. Place sausages in a saucepan, add water to cover, cover pan, and bring to a boil. Remove from heat and let stand 15 minutes. Drain, peel skin from sausages, and chop. Using a large skillet sauté mushrooms and onions in 2 tablespoons of the butter until glazed. Beat eggs until blended and mix in half-and-half cream, salt, tarragon, cheese, chopped sausage, and mushroom mixture. Turn into the pastry-lined pan and dot with butter. Bake in a 425° F. oven for 10 minutes; reduce heat to 350° F. and bake 30 minutes longer, or until set. Remove pan sides and cut into wedges to serve. Makes 8 to 10 servings.

SEAFOOD QUICHE

Press-In Pastry (preceding)
2 shallots or green onions, chopped
6 ounces cooked small shrimp
2 tablespoons butter
1 can (7-1/2 ounces) minced clams
4 eggs
1 cup half-and-half cream
1/2 teaspoon salt
1/8 teaspoon freshly grated nutmeg
5 ounces Gruyère or Swiss cheese, shredded (1-1/4 cups)

Prepare Press-In Pastry. In a skillet sauté shallots or green onions and shrimp in 1 tablespoon of the butter for 1 minute. Drain liquid from clams and reserve. Beat eggs until blended and mix in half-and-half cream, clam juice, salt, nutmeg, cheese, shrimp mixture, and clams. Turn into the pastry-lined pan and dot with remaining 1 tablespoon butter. Bake in a 425° F. oven for 10 minutes; reduce heat to 350° F. and continue baking 30 minutes longer, or until set. Remove pan sides and cut in wedges to serve. Makes 8 to 10 servings.

CHOCOLATE–DIPPED STRAWBERRIES OR TANGERINES

6 ounces semisweet chocolate
3 tablespoons orange-flavored liqueur, such as Grand Marnier or Cointreau, or strong brewed coffee
Choice of: 5 cups strawberries with stems, 8 tangerines, peeled and sectioned, or 1 pound dried apricots
Citrus, aralia, or grape leaves

In the top pan of a double boiler combine chocolate and liqueur or coffee and melt over hot water, stirring to blend. Dip berries, tangerine sections, or apricots halfway into the chocolate. Place dipped fruit on a foil-lined pan, placing berries stem end down. Chill until chocolate sets. Serve on plates lined with shiny citrus leaves or aralia or grape leaves. Makes 20 servings, with 2 or 3 pieces of fruit per person.

Greek Island Lunch, Bandit Style

SERVES THIRTY-SIX PERSONS

Cold Poached Chicken with Skordalia
Hummus with Lahvosh
Skewered Dolmas and Cherry Tomatoes
Seedless Grapes or Strawberries with Stems
Almond Cake Diamonds
Mineral Water
Wine: White Table or Chablis

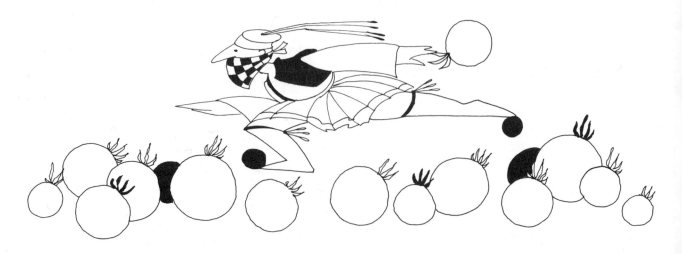

This imaginative, easy-to-prepare menu adapts to any size group. Consider it for a charity luncheon. The menu plan that follows is detailed for three dozen, but it has worked effectively for a poolside party serving one hundred twenty-five. A small group may do the cooking well in advance, or it may be parcelled out to individuals. Each plateful is dazzling, with cold chicken breasts sparked with pine-nut mayonnaise, skewered stuffed grape leaves and cherry tomatoes, garbanzo spread with bubbly Armenian cracker bread, and a feathery ground-almond cake and cluster of green grapes.

SHOPPING LIST In addition to the ingredients for the special recipes, purchase 1 bag lahvosh (Armenian cracker bread in large rounds) or sufficient sesame crackers and 4 pounds seedless grapes (red flame or Thompson) or 36 extra-large strawberries with stems.

COOK AHEAD If desired, bake the cake two or three weeks in advance and freeze it. Or bake it two or three days ahead of time. Prepare the Skordalia and Hummus and assemble the dolmas up to three days ahead of time and refrigerate. Poach and chill chicken one day in advance. For three-dozen bag lunches, prepare one cake, three recipes Skordalia, two recipes Hummus, one recipe dolmas and three dozen split chicken breasts.

SERVING LOGISTICS Arrange each luncheon on a heavy-duty paper plate with sauces in tiny containers, then wrap in plastic wrap. Slip each plate into a decorative brown or white bag, then stack the bags for swift serving. Ice the bottled water and wine in an attractive tub for help-yourself service.

COLD POACHED CHICKEN

36 split chicken breasts (about 5 ounces *each*)
1-1/2 cups chicken stock
1/2 cup dry white wine
1 teaspoon crumbled dried tarragon

Arrange 6 to 8 split chicken breasts in a large skillet. Pour in 3/4 cup of the chicken stock and 1/4 cup of the wine and season with 1/2 teaspoon of the tarragon. Cover, bring to a gentle boil, and simmer for 15 minutes, or until chicken meat turns white clear through to the bones. Remove from stock and let cool. Repeat with remaining chicken breasts, cooking them in batches and replenishing the cooking liquid as necessary with additional stock, wine, and tarragon. Remove skin and bones from chicken breasts and chill meat. Strain stock and reserve for another use. Makes 36 servings.

SKORDALIA
(Garlic Mayonnaise With Pine Nuts)

1 egg
1-1/2 tablespoons fresh lemon juice
1-1/2 tablespoons white-wine vinegar
3/4 teaspoon salt
3 garlic cloves, minced
2/3 cup safflower oil
1/3 cup olive oil
1/3 cup finely chopped lightly toasted pine nuts or almonds

Place in a blender container the egg, lemon juice, vinegar, salt, and garlic and blend a few seconds. With motor running, gradually pour in the oils in a fine, steady stream. When mixture is the consistency of mayonnaise, stir in nuts and blend 1 second. Turn into a container, cover, and refrigerate. Makes about 1-1/4 cups.

HUMMUS
(Garbanzo Bean Spread)

1 can (16 ounces) garbanzo beans, drained and liquid reserved
1/3 cup fresh lemon juice
1/3 cup tahini (sesame seed paste)
2 garlic cloves
1/4 teaspoon salt
1/4 teaspoon freshly ground black pepper
1 green onion, chopped (white part only)
3/4 teaspoon ground cumin
Cilantro or parsley sprigs
1/2 cup dry black Greek olives
Lahvosh or sesame crackers

Using a food processor fitted with a steel blade or a blender, place in the container the beans, lemon juice, tahini, garlic, salt, pepper, onion, and cumin. Blend until smooth, adding as much of the reserved bean liquid (or water) as needed to make a spreadable consistency. Turn into a bowl, cover, and chill. When ready to serve, mound in a pyramid on a plate or small footed compote and ring with cilantro or parsley sprigs and olives. Accompany with lahvosh or sesame crackers. Makes about 2 cups.

SKEWERED DOLMAS AND CHERRY TOMATOES

1 jar grape leaves or equal amount fresh grape leaves (36 to 48 leaves)
1 large onion, finely chopped
1/3 cup olive oil
1 cup short-grain white rice
1/4 cup finely chopped parsley
2 tablespoons chopped fresh dill, or 1-1/2 teaspoons crumbled dried dill
1/2 teaspoon salt
1/2 teaspoon freshly ground black pepper
1/3 cup pine nuts
1/3 cup dried currants
2 cups water
6 tablespoons fresh lemon juice
1-1/2 cups chicken stock
36 to 48 cherry tomatoes

Remove grape leaves from the jar, scald with hot water, and drain. (Or blanch fresh grape leaves in hot water for 1 minute, lift out with a slotted spoon, and drain.) Cut off stems from leaves and pat each leaf dry with paper toweling.

In a large skillet sauté onion in 2 tablespoons of the oil until golden. Add rice, parsley, dill, salt, pepper, pine nuts, currants, and 1 cup of the water. Cover and simmer 10 minutes, or until the liquid is absorbed. Remove from heat and let cool. When cool, place 1 teaspoon of the rice mixture in the center of each leaf (shiny surface down), fold sides and top in like an envelope, and roll up. (Do not roll too tightly as rice will expand.) As you make the rolls, arrange them in layers in a large Dutch oven. Sprinkle with lemon juice and remaining olive oil. Combine the chicken stock and remaining cup of water and pour over the rolls. Weight them with a baking dish, cover the Dutch oven, and simmer 35 minutes, or until rice is tender. Let cool in pan and chill until serving time. To serve, skewer together on a toothpick a dolma and a cherry tomato. Makes 36 to 48.

ALMOND CAKE DIAMONDS

6 eggs, separated
1/8 teaspoon salt
1/8 teaspoon cream of tartar
1 cup sugar
1/3 cup graham-cracker crumbs
1 teaspoon baking powder
1 teaspoon freshly grated
　 lemon peel
1/4 teaspoon almond extract
2 cups finely ground almonds
Lemon Syrup (following,
　 optional)

In a large mixing bowl beat egg whites until foamy; add salt and cream of tartar and beat until soft peaks form. Gradually add 1/4 cup of the sugar, beating until stiff, glossy peaks form. In a large mixing bowl beat egg yolks until pale yellow in color, then gradually beat in the re-maining 3/4 cup sugar, beating until thick and lemon-colored. Mix crumbs with the baking powder and lemon peel and stir into yolks. Then stir in the almond extract and half the almonds. Fold in egg whites. Gently fold in remaining nuts and turn into a buttered and floured 9- by 13-inch baking pan. Bake in a 350° F. oven for 30 minutes, or until the top springs back when touched. This cake may be served as is or, if desired, while hot pour over cooled Lemon Syrup. When cool, cut into diamond-shaped pieces. Makes 36 pieces.

LEMON SYRUP Combine in a saucepan 3/4 cup sugar, 1/3 cup water, 1/4 cup fresh lemon juice, and 2 teaspoons freshly grated lemon peel. Bring to a boil and cook, stirring, just until sugar dissolves. Let cool before pouring on cake.

INTIMATE
DINNERS
& SUPPERS

The format for staging dinner parties has made dramatic changes recently. The formality and stiffness of grandmother's era with its routine, set courses is passé. Instead, a wonderful new informality has evolved. Guests often lend a helping hand on the day of the event, or perhaps they share in advance preparations. The old-fashioned potluck idea has been updated, replaced by a thoughtfully selected dinner menu prepared cooperatively. For this, several couples may each bring a course for a special feast.

The sit-down dinner composed of several small courses is gaining popularity. It offers an atmosphere conducive to good conversation versus standing and lingering over pre-dinner cocktails. Plus match-making wine with each course increases the enjoyment.

The world's kitchens offer an endless repertoire of captivating dining themes. This menu collection hopscotches around the globe to provide a varied choice of both informal and elegant dinners. What could be more fun than to invite guests for a sampling of sausage, aïoli, strudel, or homemade pasta, or to savor a discriminating, intimate four-course French, Italian, Danish, or Belgian dinner?

SERVES EIGHT PERSONS

Cold Cucumber Soup
Salmon Mousse Ring with Béarnaise Sauce
Petite Peas and Mushrooms
Toasted Walnut and Endive Salad
Strawberry Marzipan Tart
Wine: Chardonnay or French Chablis
Coffee

Belgian Party Dinner

This pretty menu, flaunting a coral-and-green color scheme with a scarlet berry tart for dessert, makes a gala spring-time party. It is also appealing on through summer, as the salmon mousse is delectable chilled as well as hot.

SHOPPING LIST Purchase the ingredients for the special recipes.

COOK AHEAD A day in advance prepare the soup, fish ring, and the tart base. Add the berries the day of the party. Blend the béarnaise a few hours in advance and gently reheat.

SERVING LOGISTICS The dinner is designed around four sit-down courses, or, if desired, pass the soup in the garden.

COLD CUCUMBER SOUP

2 large cucumbers
2 tablespoons butter
3 green onions, chopped
4 cups chicken stock
2 tablespoons white-wine vinegar
1 teaspoon crumbled dried dill
3 tablespoons cornstarch, mixed with 3 tablespoons cold water
1/2 cup plain yogurt
1/2 cup sour cream
1/2 teaspoon white pepper
3 tablespoons chopped chives or green onion tops

Peel cucumbers, halve, scrape out any extra-large seeds, and dice. Purée in a blender or food processor. In a large saucepot melt butter, add onions, and sauté until limp. Add cucumber purée, stock, vinegar, and dill. Bring to a boil and stir in the cornstarch paste. Cook, stirring, until thickened. Remove from heat and let cool. Purée in a blender or food processor with yogurt and sour cream and season with pepper. Chill thoroughly. Taste and adjust seasoning. Serve in large-bowled wine goblets or soup bowls, with chopped chives sprinkled on top. Makes 8 to 10 servings.

SALMON MOUSSE RING

2 pounds salmon fillet,
  without skin
5 egg yolks
1 cup half-and-half cream
3/4 teaspoon salt
1/2 teaspoon crumbled dried
  tarragon
1/4 teaspoon white pepper
1 cup whipping cream
Watercress
Béarnaise Sauce (following)

Cut 1 pound of the salmon
fillet into strips 1-1/2 inches
wide and 6 inches long, making
about 8 strips. Heavily butter
a 1-1/2-quart ring mold and
line the mold with the fish
strips, spacing them about 2
inches apart around the mold.
In a blender or a food processor fitted with a steel
blade, purée the remaining
salmon fillet with egg yolks,
turn into a bowl, and stir in
half-and-half cream, salt, tarragon, and pepper. Whip cream
until stiff and fold in. Spoon
the mousse on top of the fish
fillets, spreading evenly. Tuck
any overlapping fillets down
into the mousse. Place mold
in a pan containing 1 inch
hot water and bake in a 350°
F. oven for 35 minutes, or
until set. Remove from water
bath and let cool on a rack
10 minutes. If desired, refrigerate at this point, or to serve
immediately, slip a knife around
the edge, then invert on a
platter. Garnish with watercress
and accompany with béarnaise.
If made in advance, reheat in
a pan of hot water in a 350°
F. oven for 20 minutes, or
until hot through, then unmold
as directed. Makes 8 to 10
servings.

BEARNAISE SAUCE Place in a
saucepan 1/4 cup white-wine
vinegar, 2 tablespoons dry
vermouth, 1 shallot or green
onion, chopped (white part
only), and 1 sprig parsley.
Boil until reduced to 2 tablespoons; strain. Rinse a blender
container with hot water, add
4 egg yolks, reduced vinegar
glaze, 1/2 teaspoon crumbled
dried tarragon, and 1 teaspoon
Dijon-style mustard. Blend a
few seconds. With motor running, gradually pour in 1 cup
hot melted butter, blending
until smooth. Turn into a
serving bowl. Makes about 1-
1/2 cups.

PETITE PEAS
AND MUSHROOMS

3 packages (10 ounces *each*)
  frozen petite peas, or
  6 cups shelled fresh peas
  (6 pounds, unshelled)
2 tablespoons butter
2 green onions, chopped
1/2 pound mushrooms, sliced
Salt and freshly ground black
  pepper to taste

Cook the peas in a small
amount of boiling salted water
for 3 minutes; drain. Melt
butter in a large skillet and
sauté green onions for 1
minute. Add mushrooms and
sauté 1 minute longer. Add
drained peas and stir to mix
lightly. Season with salt and
pepper. Makes 8 to 10 servings.

TOASTED WALNUT AND ENDIVE SALAD

1 bunch watercress, stems removed
2 bunches Belgian endive, separated into leaves and sliced
2 heads butter lettuce, torn into bite-sized pieces
1/2 cup olive or safflower oil
3 tablespoons red-wine vinegar
2 teaspoons Dijon-style mustard
1/2 teaspoon salt
1/4 teaspoon freshly ground black pepper
2 tablespoons chopped shallots or green onions (white part only)
1 teaspoon chopped fresh tarragon, or 1/4 teaspoon crumbled dried tarragon
1/2 cup toasted walnut pieces

Place in a salad bowl the watercress, endive, and lettuce. Stir together the oil, vinegar, mustard, salt, pepper, shallots or green onions, and tarragon. Pour over greens and mix lightly. Scatter over the nuts. Makes 8 servings.

STRAWBERRY MARZIPAN TART

11-inch prebaked fluted Tart Shell (following)
1/2 cup almond paste
1/4 cup powdered sugar
2 tablespoons butter, at room temperature
1 egg white
1/4 teaspoon almond extract
1 quart strawberries, hulled, or 3 cups strawberries, hulled, and 2 kiwi fruit, peeled and sliced
1/3 cup puréed apricot preserves
Sweetened whipped cream (optional)

Prepare the pastry shell. Beat together until blended the almond paste, powdered sugar, butter, egg white, and almond extract. Spread over the cooled pastry shell. Just before serving, arrange berries in a pretty design on the filling, or encircle the berries with a ring of kiwi. Heat apricot purée until it melts and drizzle over the fruit. Chill. If desired, serve with sweetened whipped cream. Makes 10 servings.

TART SHELL Place in a mixing bowl 1 cup all-purpose flour, 1/4 pound (1/2 cup) butter, and 2 tablespoons powdered sugar. Mix until crumbly. Pat onto the bottom and sides of a fluted 11-inch flan pan. Refrigerate 15 minutes to firm up, or freeze 5 minutes. Bake in a 425° F. oven for 8 minutes, or until golden brown. Let cool on a wire rack before filling. Makes one 11-inch shell.

NOTE When berries are out of season, fresh pineapple, diced, makes a refreshing stand-in.

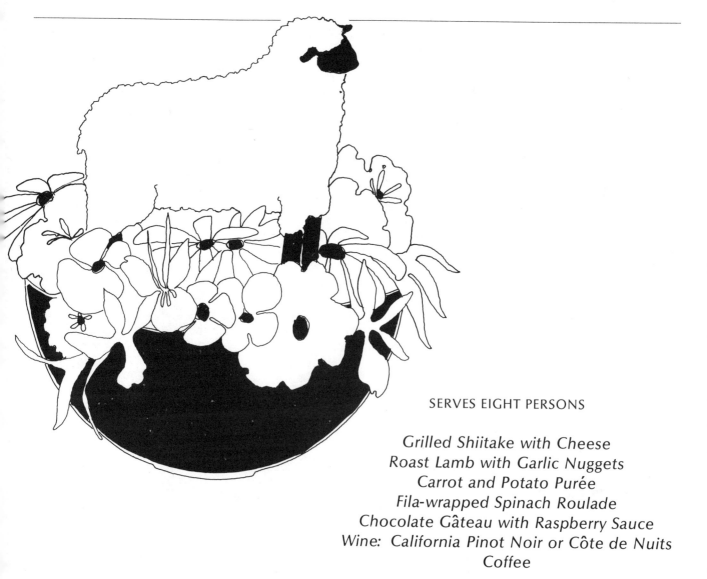

SERVES EIGHT PERSONS

Grilled Shiitake with Cheese
Roast Lamb with Garlic Nuggets
Carrot and Potato Purée
Fila-wrapped Spinach Roulade
Chocolate Gâteau with Raspberry Sauce
Wine: California Pinot Noir or Côte de Nuits
Coffee

Easy Elegant French Dinner

This elegant party meal goes together with aplomb when the vegetable roulade and dessert are made in advance. The first course features exotic shiitake mushrooms hot, cloaked in cheese. Rare roast lamb with sweet garlic morsels, a golden vegetable purée, and a crispy pastry roll of spinach punctuated with blue cheese fill the entrée plate. A soufflélike chocolate cake with cream and berry purée makes an enthralling finale.

SHOPPING LIST Purchase the ingredients for the special recipes.

COOK AHEAD Bake the cake a day or two in advance or two or three weeks ahead and freeze. Let warm to room temperature before serving. Assemble the fila roll and bake a day ahead, if desired. The other components of the menu are swift to assemble.

SERVING LOGISTICS Serve in three courses. Present the mushroom first course with the white wine. Continue with a red wine to complement the entrée.

GRILLED SHIITAKE WITH CHEESE

8 fresh shiitake mushrooms or regular white mushrooms, about 2 to 2-1/2 inches in diameter
6 tablespoons butter
1/2 cup finely chopped parsley
3 garlic cloves, finely minced
1 teaspoon crumbled dried tarragon
2 breakfast cheeses, thinly sliced horizontally in 4 slices each, or 1 round chèvre cheese, cut in 8 slices
Freshly ground black pepper

Pull off mushroom stems and chop. Slice each mushroom cap in 4 or 5 slices, keeping the slices together so that they retain the shape of a whole mushroom. Arrange sliced caps on a well-buttered baking pan and tuck the chopped mushroom stems on top of each. Melt the butter and mix in parsley, garlic, and tarragon. Scatter butter mixture over the mushrooms. Bake in a 425° F. oven for 5 minutes. Arrange a slice of cheese on top of each mushroom and sprinkle with pepper. Continue baking for 5 minutes longer, or until cheese melts. Serve at once on individual plates. Makes 8 servings.

ROAST LAMB WITH GARLIC NUGGETS

4- to 5-pound leg of lamb
Salt and freshly ground black
   pepper
1 teaspoon dried oregano leaves
2 large heads garlic
2 teaspoons butter
3 lemons
Rosemary sprigs or mint sprigs

Season the lamb leg with salt and pepper and rub oregano over the cut surfaces. Insert a meat thermometer in the thickest part. Place on a rack in a roasting pan and roast in a 425° F. oven for 25 minutes, or until browned. Reduce temperature to 325° F. and continue roasting until meat thermometer registes 140° F. for medium-rare meat, about 1-1/2 to 1-3/4 hours. Place on a carving board and let rest for 15 minutes for the juices to set up.

  Meanwhile, separate garlic heads into cloves but do not peel. Place in a saucepan, cover with water, bring to a boil and let simmer 5 minutes. Drain and repeat this process twice. Drain thoroughly and let cool. Slip off the skins. Sauté the garlic cloves in butter for 2 to 3 minutes or until lightly browned. Place in a little bowl beside the roast lamb. Cut lemons in half zigzag style and arrange on the board with rosemary or mint sprigs. Carve meat and accompany each serving with 2 or 3 browned garlic cloves. Makes about 8 servings.

CARROT AND POTATO PUREE

6 large carrots, peeled and
   diced
4 medium potatoes, peeled
   and cut in 1-inch cubes
2 tablespoons butter
2 to 3 tablespoons whipping
   cream or milk, or as needed
1/4 teaspoon salt
1/4 teaspoon white pepper
1/4 teaspoon ground nutmeg

In a large saucepan cook carrots and potatoes in boiling salted water, covered, until very tender, about 15 minutes. Drain. Place in a food processor fitted with a steel blade and process with butter, cream or milk, and seasonings. (Or purée in a blender.) If necessary, add a little more cream or milk to achieve the desired fluffy consistency. Makes 8 servings.

FILA–WRAPPED SPINACH ROULADE

4 tablespoons (1/4 cup) butter
1 medium yellow onion,
   chopped
1 bunch (about 6) green
   onions, chopped
2 large bunches spinach,
   trimmed and finely chopped
1/3 cup chopped parsley
1/4 teaspoon salt
1/4 teaspoon freshly ground
   black pepper
1/2 teaspoon crumbled dried
   tarragon
4 ounces blue cheese, cut in
   chunks or coarsely crumbled
1/2 cup shredded Jarlsberg or
   Swiss cheese
2 eggs, beaten
5 sheets fila dough

In a large skillet, melt 1 tablespoon of the butter and sauté the yellow and green onions until limp. Add the spinach and heat until just wilted; let cool and drain off any moisture. Place in a large bowl the spinach and onions, parsley, salt, pepper, tarragon, blue cheese, Jarlsberg or Swiss cheese, and eggs and mix lightly. Melt the remaining 3 tablespoons butter. Lay out 1 sheet of fila (keep remaining sheets covered with plastic wrap so they don't dry out) and brush lightly with melted butter. Cover with a second sheet, butter lightly, and repeat the layering with remaining sheets, lightly buttering each one. Spoon spinach mixture in a log shape along a long side, leaving a 1-inch strip uncovered along edge and at sides. Fold in 1-inch sides of fila and roll up the dough like a jelly roll, encasing the spinach. Place seam side down on a lightly buttered baking pan. Lightly brush top of fila roll with melted butter.

Bake in a 375° F. oven for 40 minutes, or until crispy and browned. Cut in 8 slices and serve warm. Makes 8 servings.

CHOCOLATE GATEAU WITH RASPBERRY SAUCE

8 ounces semisweet chocolate
1/4 pound (1/2 cup) butter
6 eggs, separated
1/8 teaspoon salt
1/8 teaspoon cream of tartar
3/4 cup sugar
1 teaspoon vanilla extract
Whipped cream or vanilla ice
   cream (optional)
6 tablespoons all-purpose flour
Raspberry Sauce (following)

In the top pan of a double boiler, combine the chocolate and butter and melt over hot water, stirring to blend. Let cool. Beat egg whites until foamy, add salt and cream of tartar and beat until soft peaks form.

Add 3 tablespoons of the sugar and beat until stiff, glossy peaks form. Beat egg yolks until thick and lemon-colored and beat in remaining sugar and vanilla extract. Stir in chocolate mixture. Fold in one-third of the whites to lighten the mixture. Then gently fold in flour and remaining whites. Turn into a buttered and floured 9-inch spring-form pan. Bake in a 350° F. oven for 35 minutes or until set 3 inches in from the pan edges; the center should still be moist. Turn off heat and let cool in oven 10 minutes with door ajar. Remove from oven and place on a wire rack to cool. To serve, remove pan sides and cut in wedges. Garnish with whipped cream or ice cream and Raspberry Sauce. Makes 8 to 10 servings.

RASPBERRY SAUCE Thaw 1 package (10 ounces) frozen raspberries. Purée in a blender and then press through a wire sieve, discarding seeds.

Austrian Dinner

This intimate, elite dinner for six is a joy for a guest meal because both the strudel entrée and cake may be made well in advance. The other elements go together swiftly.

SHOPPING LIST Purchase the ingredients for the special recipes and the lettuce and cheese for the salad course.

COOK AHEAD Assemble the strudels a day in advance and refrigerate or up to two or three weeks ahead and freeze. Bake the cake a day or two ahead and refrigerate, or up to two or three weeks ahead and freeze. Stuff the eggs early in the day.

SERVING LOGISTICS Present in four courses at the table. If desired, accompany the salad course with a platter of brie or chèvre.

SERVES SIX PERSONS

Eggs with Caviar
Chicken and Leek Strudels
Asparagus with Browned Butter
Butter Lettuce Salad with Brie or Chèvre
Royal Chocolate Almond Cake
Wine: Johannisberg Riesling,
White Zinfandel, or Gamay Beaujolais Nouveau
Coffee

EGGS WITH CAVIAR

6 eggs, hard-cooked
2 tablespoons mayonnaise
2 tablespoons sour cream
1/4 teaspoon salt
1/4 teaspoon white pepper
1 teaspoon Dijon-style mustard
1 jar (2 ounces) lumpfish caviar
Watercress sprigs

Halve eggs lengthwise and transfer yolks to a bowl. Add mayonnaise, sour cream, salt, pepper, and mustard to yolks and mix well. Pile into egg white halves. Cover and refrigerate. At serving time, arrange 2 stuffed egg halves on each of 6 small plates and spoon caviar over the yolk filling. Tuck a sprig of watercress on each plate. Makes 6 servings.

ASPARAGUS WITH BROWNED BUTTER

2 pounds asparagus
1/4 cup sweet (unsalted) butter
3 tablespoons finely chopped parsley

Trim ends from asparagus. With a vegetable peeler trim off the tough outer skin on the lower part of the stalks. Cook in a large pot of boiling salted water until crisp tender, about 5 to 7 minutes; drain. Heat butter in a small pan until it bubbles and starts to brown slightly. Pour over asparagus. Sprinkle with parsley. Makes 6 servings.

CHICKEN AND LEEK STRUDELS

3-pound broiler chicken, roasted and chilled, or 6 split chicken breasts, cooked
5 tablespoons butter
1 bunch (about 3) leeks, chopped (white part only)
1 carrot, peeled and shredded
1/4 cup chopped parsley
3/4 teaspoon crumbled dried tarragon
1/4 teaspoon white pepper
1/4 teaspoon salt
2 eggs, beaten
5 ounces Jarlsberg or Gruyère cheese, shredded (1-1/4 cups)
6 sheets fila dough

Remove skin and bones from chicken and dice meat in large chunks. Place chicken meat in a bowl. In a large skillet melt 1 tablespoon of the butter and sauté leeks and carrot until soft. Add to the chicken along with the parsley, tarragon, pepper, salt, eggs, and cheese and mix lightly. Melt the remaining 4 tablespoons butter. Lay out 1 sheet of fila (keep remaining sheets covered with plastic wrap so they don't dry out), brush half of it lightly with melted butter, and fold sheet in half. Brush top of folded sheet lightly with butter. Place one-sixth of the filling in a log shape along a long side, leaving a 1-inch strip uncovered along edge and at sides. Fold in 1-inch sides and roll up the dough like a jelly roll, encasing the filling. Place seam side down on a lightly buttered baking sheet. Repeat with remaining fila sheets and filling. Lightly brush tops of fila rolls with butter. At this point, cover and refrigerate or freeze. Let thaw completely before baking. Bake in a 375° F. oven for 20 minutes, or until golden brown. Makes 6 servings.

ROYAL CHOCOLATE ALMOND CAKE

5 eggs, separated
1 cup plus 2 tablespoons firmly packed brown sugar
1 teaspoon vanilla extract
1/4 teaspoon almond extract
1-1/2 cups finely ground almonds, filberts, or pecans, or a combination
4 ounces semisweet chocolate, grated (2/3 cup)
2 teaspoons freshly grated orange peel
1/8 teaspoon salt
1/8 teaspoon cream of tartar
Strawberries and/or whipped cream

Beat egg yolks until thick and lemon-colored and beat in 1 cup of the sugar and vanilla and almond extracts until thick. Mix together the nuts, chocolate, and orange peel and fold in half the mixture. Beat egg whites until foamy, add salt and cream of tartar, and beat until soft peaks form. Add the remaining 2 tablespoons sugar and beat until stiff, glossy peaks form. Fold one-third of the whites into the yolks to lighten them. Fold in remaining nut and chocolate mixture and gently fold in remaining whites. Turn into an ungreased 9-inch springform pan. Bake in a 350° F. oven for 30 to 35 minutes, or until the top springs back when touched lightly. Remove from the oven and let cool upside down on a wire rack. Cut in wedges and accompany with strawberries and/or whipped cream. Makes 8 to 10 servings.

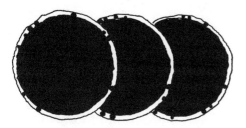 

SERVES EIGHT PERSONS

Choucroute Garnie
Pickles and Mustards
Sourdough French Bread or Baguettes and Sweet Butter
Apple Basket, Roasted Chestnuts, and Cheese Tray
or
Apple-Almond Cake
Wine: Alsatian Riesling or California Gewürztraminer
Coffee

Alsatian Sausage-Sampling Party

The fascinating variety of sausages available in the marketplace offers a fine excuse for a party theme. A sampling of sausages can be incorporated with the famous Alsatian dish, choucroute garnie, meaning sauerkraut with all its trimmings.

This menu is appropriate for an informal party with friends. It also suits a ski-country dinner or beach party. The classic Alsatian dish itself is the meal, rounded out with complementary accompaniments like dill pickles, assorted mustards, and French bread. In season, one option is to finish off with chestnuts roasted over fireplace coals. Pass apples, to savor out of hand, and a tray of cheeses. As an alternative, a caramelized apple-almond cake makes a glorious finale.

SHOPPING LIST Buy the ingredients for the special recipes, plus a selection of at least three kinds of mustards, assorted pickles, French bread or baguettes, sweet butter, and chestnuts, apples, and two or three cheeses, such as brie, Gruyère, and Danish blue Castello or Oregon blue, if you have opted for that menu choice.

COOK AHEAD Plan to bake the cake a day in advance, if desired. Cook the sauerkraut a day ahead, also, as reheating only enhances its flavors. With this done, table setting is the prime task on the party day.

SERVING LOGISTICS Set up a buffet so guests help themselves and are free to return for additional sampling.

CHOUCROUTE GARNIE

3 pounds sauerkraut
2 slices salt pork or thickly
   sliced bacon
1 large onion, thinly sliced
1 pound pork loin, sliced,
   or smoked pork chops
2 tart cooking apples, such as
   pippin, Jonathan, or golden
   delicious

1 small smoked ham hock
   (about 3/4 pound)
1 bay leaf
3 whole cloves
4 black peppercorns
1-1/2 cups dry white wine
2 pounds assorted sausages:
   bratwurst, knackwurst,
   kielbasa, veal frankfurters,
   cocktail frankfurters, or
   Italian garlic sausages

Turn sauerkraut into a metal strainer, rinse thoroughly under cold running water, and drain well. Dice salt pork or bacon and sauté in a large 4- to 6-quart flameproof casserole. Add onion to casserole and sauté in drippings until golden brown. Add pork loin or chops and brown. Add the sauerkraut, whole apples, ham hock, bay leaf, cloves, peppercorns, and wine. Cover and bake in a 325° F. oven for 2-1/2 hours. Add sausages, spooning some of juices over them. Continue baking 30 minutes longer, or until sausages are thoroughly heated. To serve, mound sauerkraut on a hot platter. Top with pork loin or chops and skinned ham hock. Surround with sausages. Makes 8 servings.

APPLE–ALMOND CAKE

4 large golden delicious
   apples
1/2 cup water
3/4 cup sugar
1/4 pound (1/2 cup) butter,
   at room temperature
2 eggs
1/4 teaspoon almond extract
1 cup finely ground almonds
1 tablespoon all-purpose flour
Vanilla ice cream or whipped
   cream

Peel and core apples and cut in wedges. Place in a large skillet with water and 1/4 cup of the sugar. Cover and simmer 5 minutes; remove cover and continue cooking 5 minutes longer, letting juices evaporate; set aside.

In a mixing bowl beat butter until creamy and beat in the remaining 1/2 cup sugar and eggs, beating until smooth. Mix in almond extract, nuts, and flour. Spread batter in a buttered and floured 9-inch spring-form pan. Arrange apple wedges in a pinwheel pattern on top. Bake in a 350° F. oven for 30 minutes, or until golden brown. Serve warm with ice cream or whipped cream. Makes 8 servings.

Spanish Parador Dinner

SERVES EIGHT PERSONS

Clams on the Half Shell
Boned Stuffed Lamb
Broccoli Flowerets with Browned Garlic
Orange and Watercress Salad
Flan with Strawberries
Wine: Sauvignon Blanc, Muscadet, or White Rioja
and California Barbera or Spanish Red Rioja
Coffee

This festive menu suits a gala occasion. A seafood first course, delectable sausage-stuffed lamb entrée, and caramelized flan dessert make it ideal for a celebration.

SHOPPING LIST Purchase the ingredients for the special recipes, plus about 2 pounds of broccoli.

COOK AHEAD Make the caramelized custard a day in advance, if desired. Assemble the lamb a day ahead, as well, or early on the day of the dinner. Compose the salad several hours ahead, then dress at the last minute.

SERVING LOGISTICS Present in three courses in the dining room, commencing with seafood and white wine as the first course. Carve the roast lamb at the table The salad may accompany the entrée.

CLAMS ON THE HALF SHELL

Purchase 3 or 4 butter or rock cockle clams per person. Wash thoroughly, scrubbing the shells. Pry open, arrange on individual plates, and serve well chilled on the half shell with lemon wedges.

BONED STUFFED LAMB

2 tablespoons butter
1 large onion, finely chopped
2 carrots, peeled and finely chopped
1 pound bulk mild Italian sausage
3 garlic cloves, minced
1/2 teaspoon crumbled dried oregano
4 slices egg bread or other fine-grained white bread, cubed
1 leg of lamb, boned and butterflied (about 4 to 5 pounds, American or frozen New Zealand, thawed)
1/2 teaspoon salt
1/2 teaspoon freshly ground black pepper
Rosemary sprigs
Lemons

Melt butter in a large skillet and sauté onion and carrots until golden brown; remove from pan and set aside. Add sausage and sauté until crisp and crumbly; pour off drippings. Add garlic, oregano, bread, and sautéed vegetables to the sausage and mix lightly. Lay out meat flat, cover evenly with stuffing, roll, and tie with string to make a compact roll. Season with salt and pepper. Place on a rack in a roasting pan and insert a meat thermometer. Roast in a 325° F. oven until meat thermometer registers 140° F. for medium-rare meat or 150° F. for medium meat, about 1-1/2 to 1-3/4 hours. Place on a platter and ring with rosemary sprigs. Halve the lemons zigzag style and arrange on platter with lamb. Makes 8 to 10 servings.

ORANGE AND WATERCRESS SALAD

1 bunch watercress or curly endive
6 oranges, peeled to remove all white membrane and thinly sliced
1/2 cup pimiento-stuffed olives
1 medium sweet red onion, thinly sliced and separated into rings
1/4 cup olive oil
1/4 cup safflower oil
1 teaspoon freshly grated lemon peel
1/3 cup orange juice
1 tablespoon fresh lemon juice
1/2 teaspoon salt
1/2 teaspoon paprika
1/2 teaspoon dry mustard

Line a large platter with sprigs of watercress or endive and arrange orange slices in an overlapping pattern on top. Scatter over olives and onion rings. Cover with plastic wrap and refrigerate until ready to serve. For dressing, shake together the oils, lemon peel, orange juice, lemon juice, salt, paprika, and mustard. Pour over salad. Makes 8 servings.

FLAN WITH STRAWBERRIES

Caramel-lined pan (following)
3-1/2 cups milk
4 eggs
4 egg yolks
2/3 cup granulated sugar
2 teaspoons vanilla extract
3 cups strawberries, hulled
3 tablespoons kirsch or Grand Marnier
3 tablespoons powdered sugar
1 cup whipping cream, whipped with sugar and kirsch or Grand Marnier to taste (optional)

Prepare the caramel-lined pan. Scald milk. Beat together the eggs and egg yolks until blended and beat in the granulated sugar, vanilla extract, and hot milk. Pour into the caramel-lined pan. Place in a pan containing 1 inch of hot water and bake in a 325° F. oven for 1 hour, or until the custard is set. Remove from the water bath, let cool, and chill. Loosen caramel custard with a knife and invert on a platter. Toss berries with liqueur and powdered sugar and spoon in the center of the ring. Spoon whipped cream in a bowl and serve alongside, if desired. Makes 8 to 10 servings.

CARAMEL-LINED PAN Heat 1/3 cup sugar in a heavy saucepan until it melts, caramelizes, and turns amber. Immediately pour into a 1-1/2-quart ring mold, swirling pan to coat.

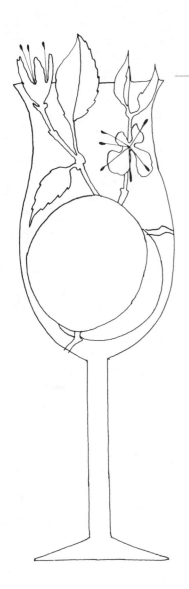

Pistachio Dip with Vegetable Basket
Wine Broth with Pesto
Spiedini
Green Beans with Herbs
Spinach Salad with Toasted Pine Nuts
Strawberry-and-Kiwi-topped Lemon Tart
Wine: Barbera, Nebbiolo, or Chianti Classico
Coffee

The fresh bounty of a true Italian kitchen flavors this vibrantly colored dinner. It is ideal for all seasons. It also adapts well as a portable meal at a beach home or in ski country. The entrée features neat meat rolls encasing cheese and salami that may be barbecued or broiled. Dessert offers a dazzling fruit tart.

SHOPPING LIST Purchase the ingredients for the special recipes.

COOK AHEAD A day in advance make the mayonnaise dip and dessert tart. Assemble the meat rolls early in the day.

SERVING LOGISTICS Let the Pistachio Dip and assorted vegetables compose the appetizer along with aperitifs. Then present the dinner at the table in four courses: soup, entrée, salad, and dessert.

PISTACHIO DIP WITH VEGETABLE BASKET

1 egg
1-1/2 tablespoons fresh lemon juice
1-1/2 tablespoons white-wine vinegar
3/4 teaspoon salt
3/4 teaspoon dry mustard
7/8 cup safflower oil (or part olive oil)
1 garlic clove, chopped
1/2 cup chopped spinach
2 tablespoons chopped parsley
1/2 teaspoon crumbled dried tarragon
1/2 cup pistachios
Assorted vegetables in a basket: mushrooms, fennel, red pepper, cherry tomatoes, cauliflower, pea pods, zucchini, carrots

Place in a blender container or food processor fitted with a steel blade the egg, lemon juice, vinegar, salt, and mustard. With motor running, gradually pour in oil and blend until smooth. Add garlic, spinach, parsley, tarragon, and nuts and blend a few seconds longer, or until sauce is flecked green. Turn into a serving bowl and chill. Accompany with a basket of vegetables cut for dipping. Makes about 1-1/2 cups sauce.

GREEN BEANS WITH HERBS

2 pounds slender green beans
2 tablespoons butter
2 tablespoons chopped parsley
1 garlic clove, minced
2 teaspoons chopped fresh tarragon, or 1/2 teaspoon crumbled dried tarragon

Trim ends from beans. If the beans are slender, leave whole. If unable to purchase slender ones, cut in half lengthwise, if desired. Cook beans in a large pot of boiling salted water until crisp tender, about 5 to 7 minutes; drain. Add butter, parsley, garlic, and tarragon and heat, shaking pan to coat beans. Makes 8 servings.

WINE BROTH WITH PESTO

2 tablespoons butter, at room temperature
1/3 cup grated Romano cheese
2 garlic cloves, minced
3 tablespoons chopped fresh basil
1 tablespoon chopped parsley
6 cups beef stock
1/2 cup dry red wine

To make the pesto mix together in a small bowl the butter, cheese, garlic, basil, and parsley. Heat stock and wine until steaming. Ladle into 8 small bowls or cups and add a dollop of pesto to each. Makes 8 servings.

SPIEDINI

2-1/2-pound sirloin tip roast,
  sliced 3/16 inch thick,
  or 2-1/2 pounds thinly
  sliced veal cutlets
1/2 teaspoon salt
1/2 teaspoon freshly ground
  black pepper
1 teaspoon crumbled dried
  oregano
8 ounces Monterey jack or
  Provolone cheese, thinly
  sliced
5 ounces thinly sliced salami or
  prosciutto
2 tablespoons olive oil
1 garlic clove, minced

Pound meat between 2 sheets
of waxed paper until very
thin, then cut the sirloin into
rectangles about 3 by 5 inches.
The veal cutlets can be
pounded to these dimensions.
Sprinkle with salt, pepper,
and oregano. Lay a slice of
cheese and one of salami or
prosciutto on each slice of
meat. Roll up from narrow
end. Thread 2 or 3 meat rolls
on a skewer. Combine oil
and garlic and brush over
meat. Broil or grill over medium-
hot coals, turning to brown
all sides. Makes 8 servings.

NOTE If desired, cut French
bread into strips the size of
the meat rolls and roll in
melted butter, seasoned with
minced garlic. Skewer and
broil alongside meat.

SPINACH SALAD
WITH TOASTED PINE NUTS

1/2 cup olive oil
1/4 cup red-wine vinegar
1 garlic clove, minced
1/2 teaspoon salt
1/2 teaspoon freshly ground
  black pepper
2 teaspoons Dijon-style
  mustard
2 cups cherry tomatoes
2 bunches spinach, trimmed
2 eggs, hard-cooked and
  sieved
1/4 cup toasted pine nuts

Mix together in a small bowl
the oil, vinegar, garlic, salt,
pepper, and mustard. Add
cherry tomatoes and let stand
1 hour. Tear spinach into
bite-size pieces and place in
a bowl. Pour over dressing
and tomatoes and mix lightly.
Scatter over eggs and shower
with nuts. Makes 8 servings.

STRAWBERRY–AND–KIWI–
TOPPED LEMON TART

11-inch prebaked fluted Tart
  Shell (page 57)
8 ounces cream cheese, at
  room temperature
3/4 cup sugar
3 eggs
2 teaspoons freshly grated
  lemon peel
1/2 cup fresh lemon juice
2 kiwi fruit, peeled and sliced
1 basket strawberries, hulled
1/4 cup puréed apricot
  preserves

Prepare the pastry shell. In a
mixing bowl beat the cheese
until creamy and beat in sugar,
eggs, and lemon peel and
juice. Pour into the baked
pastry shell and bake in a
350° F. oven for 20 minutes,
or until set. Let cool and chill.
Arrange kiwi slices in a circle
on top. Place strawberries in
the center of the circle in a
decorative design. Heat apricot
purée until it melts and drizzle
over the fruit. Chill. Cut into
wedges to serve. Makes 10
servings.

Pasta-Making Party

SERVES EIGHT PERSONS

Roasted Italian Sausages with Peppers
Mediterranean-style Olives
Pasta
Pasta Sauces: Carbonara, Pesto, and Fresh Tomato
Bread Sticks   Green Salad
Cheese Tray: Gorgonzola and Bel Paese
Crenshaw Melon Wedges and Ladyfinger Grapes
Wine: Zinfandel, Petite Sirah, or Côte de Rhône
Espresso or Coffee

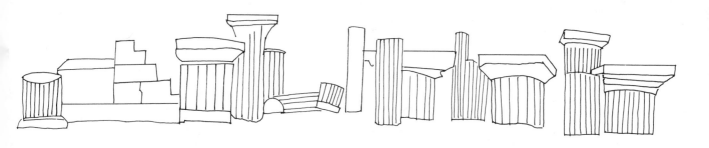

A pasta-making party is a festive way to enjoy an evening with close friends and to savor a delectable Italian repast. The emphasis of the feast is the joyful task of cranking out egg pasta and serving it with a trio of sauces. Roasted crispy sausages make a succulent, simple starter, along with oil-cured olives. Finish off with cheese and fruit.

SHOPPING LIST Purchase the ingredients for the special recipes, plus olives, bread sticks, salad greens, fruits, and cheeses. If fresh basil is out of season, concentrate on the other two sauces.

COOK AHEAD If desired, mix the pasta dough in advance, ready for the guests to crank.

SERVING LOGISTICS This informal meal may be served in the kitchen or the dining room.

ROASTED ITALIAN SAUSAGES WITH PEPPERS

1 pound mild Italian sausages
2 red bell peppers (optional)

With a fork prick the surface of the sausages in about four places. Place in a baking pan. If peppers are available, cut into sixths and remove seeds. Arrange pepper slices in the pan with the sausages. Bake in a 350° F. oven for 45 minutes, turning once. Slice sausages in 3/4-inch pieces and serve on a platter with peppers, to skewer with toothpicks. Makes 8 appetizer servings.

PASTA

DOUGH
2 cups all-purpose flour
3/4 teaspoon salt
2 eggs, lightly beaten
1 tablespoon olive oil
About 3 tablespoons warm
   water

FOR COOKING
6 quarts water
1 tablespoon salt
1 tablespoon olive oil

If mixing by hand, place flour and salt in a mixing bowl, make a well in the center, and add the eggs, oil, and 1 tablespoon of the water. Mix with a spoon or hands, adding more water, several drops at a time, until dough forms a firm ball. If using a heavy-duty mixer instead, place all ingredients in mixing bowl without beating eggs first and mix until dough clings together in a ball. Let rest, covered with plastic wrap, for 30 minutes.

Knead and roll pasta following pasta machine directions. Cut into desired widths, for tagliarini (thin noodles) or fettuccine (wide noodles). To cook, bring water, salt, and olive oil to a boil in a large kettle. Add pasta and boil it 3 minutes or until just tender—al dente; do not overcook. Drain and dress with choice of sauce. Make 2 recipes in 2 batches for 8 servings.

PESTO SAUCE

1-1/2 cups lightly packed
   fresh basil leaves
1/3 cup olive oil
2 garlic cloves
1/4 cup pine nuts or walnuts
1/2 cup freshly grated Romano
   cheese

Place in a food processor
fitted with a steel blade or in
a blender container the basil,
oil, garlic, nuts, and grated
cheese. Process until smoothly
blended. To serve, toss with
hot cooked pasta, preferably
fettuccine. Makes about 1-
1/2 cups sauce, enough for 2
recipes of pasta.

FRESH TOMATO SAUCE

2 large onions, chopped
2 tablespoons olive oil
3 garlic cloves, minced
12 large ripe tomatoes, peeled
   and chopped
1/2 teaspoon salt
1/2 teaspoon freshly ground
   black pepper
1/2 cup chopped fresh basil
3 tablespoons finely chopped
   parsley
Freshly grated Parmesan or
   Romano cheese

Using a large skillet, sauté
onions in oil until limp. Add
garlic, tomatoes, salt, and
pepper and simmer, uncov-
ered, stirring occasionally, for
20 minutes, or until reduced
to a saucelike consistency.
Add basil and simmer 5 minutes longer. Toss with 1 recipe
of hot cooked pasta, cut in
either tagliarini or fettuccine
width, using as much of the
sauce as desired. Sprinkle
with parsley and pass grated
cheese. Makes about 3 cups
sauce.

CARBONARA SAUCE

6 strips bacon, cut in 1-inch
   pieces
1 large onion, chopped
2 egg yolks
6 ounces Monterey jack or
   white Cheddar cheese,
   shredded (1-1/2 cups)
2/3 cup julienne-cut
   prosciutto or salami
1/2 cup chopped parsley

In a large skillet sauté bacon
until crisp; remove from pan.
Drain off all but 2 tablespoons
drippings. Add onion and sauté
until limp. In a bowl beat egg
yolks until light and mix in
cheese, prosciutto or salami,
parsley, onion, and bacon. To
serve, add 1 recipe of the hot
cooked tagliarini and mix
lightly. Makes 8 servings.

SERVES FOUR PERSONS

Aïoli with Shrimp, Hard-cooked Eggs, and Vegetables
Crusty French Bread and Sweet Butter
Cheese Provençal or Herb-coated Boursin
Hot Pears with Caramel Sauce
Coffee or Espresso
Wine: Sauvignon Blanc, Pinot Blanc, or Verdicchio

Aïoli Party Supper

The rustic and robust Provençal garlic mayonnaise called aïoli is the centerpiece of this easy supper. Guests enjoy dipping into it the garden vegetables, shrimp, and eggs. Cheese and an ultra-easy fruit dessert complete this almost-instant spread.

SHOPPING LIST Purchase the ingredients for the special recipes, plus the French bread and sweet butter.

COOK AHEAD Flavor the cheese three or four days in advance or buy the cheese. Prepare the aïoli a day or two in advance and refrigerate. Caramelize the pears just before serving as they are fast to prepare, or if preferred, do a day ahead and reheat.

SERVING LOGISTICS Serve each guest an individual bowl of garlic mayonnaise in a stoneware dish or small bowl. Arrange the accompaniments in one large serving bowl or on individual plates. The cheese and dessert may follow as separate courses.

AIOLI WITH SHRIMP, HARD–COOKED EGGS, AND VEGETABLES

1 egg
2 tablespoons white-wine vinegar
1 tablespoon fresh lemon juice
3/4 teaspoon salt
1 teaspoon Dijon-style mustard
4 or 5 garlic cloves
1/2 cup olive oil
1/2 cup safflower oil
Accompaniments: 1 pound cooked and shelled medium shrimp, 4 hard-cooked eggs, 1 basket cherry tomatoes, 4 cooked artichokes, 1/2 pound mushrooms, 1 head fennel, separated into stalks

To prepare aïoli, place in a blender container or food processor the egg, vinegar, lemon juice, salt, mustard, and garlic and blend until smooth. With motor running, gradually pour in oils in a fine, steady stream, blending to make a thick mayonnaise. Turn into a sauce bowl, cover, and chill. Makes about 1-1/4 cups.

To serve, arrange on a large platter or individual plates the shrimp, eggs, tomatoes, artichokes, mushrooms, and fennel. Spoon the aïoli into individual sauce dishes. Makes 4 servings.

CHEESE PROVENCAL

8 ounces Monterey jack or fontina cheese
1 tablespoon dried herbs from Provence (thyme, savory, oregano, and rosemary)
1 dried hot red chili pepper, split
1 bay leaf
Virgin olive oil (about 1 cup)

Cut cheese in 1-1/4-inch cubes and place in a wide-mouthed jar. Sprinkle with herbs. Add chili pepper and bay leaf. Pour in oil to just cover cheese. Cover and let stand for 3 or 4 days, or longer. Accompany with thin wheat crackers or serve on small plates with a fork. Makes 4 servings.

HOT PEARS IN CARAMEL SAUCE

4 anjou or Bartlett pears
2 tablespoons butter
1/4 cup sugar
1/3 cup whipping cream
Vanilla or coffee ice cream or whipped cream (optional)

Peel pears and core the bases, leaving stems intact. Melt butter in a shallow baking dish or pie pan in a 425° F. oven. Roll pears in the butter and sprinkle them with sugar. Bake for 15 to 20 minutes, or until the sugar caramelizes and mixture turns amber. Pour in the cream and blend with the syrupy sauce. Continue baking for 15 minutes longer, basting pears with sauce twice, until sauce turns a rich amber color. Let cool slightly. Serve warm in dessert bowls with ice cream or whipped cream, if desired. Makes 4 servings.

This Nordic menu is beautifully geared for make-ahead ease. The appetizer, soup, entrée, and dessert may be done a day in advance. In fact, the nut torte freezes well, if desired. For a starter, offer the decorative caviar and egg bowl. The vegetable soup, chicken rolls, and elegant almond cake glazed with chocolate compose a menu popular with all ages.

SERVES EIGHT PERSONS

Caviar Torte
Tomato Soup with Chives
Tivoli Chicken and Ham Rolls
Glazed Carrots
Butter Lettuce Salad (optional)
Chocolate-glazed Marzipan Torte
Wine: Chenin Blanc or Zinfandel Rosé
Coffee

SHOPPING LIST Purchase the ingredients for the special recipes, plus lettuce for the salad, if serving.

COOK AHEAD Plan to make the appetizer, soup, and chicken rolls a day in advance. The cake may be done a day or two in advance or two or three weeks ahead and frozen.

SERVING LOGISTICS Present the caviar mold as an appetizer, then follow with three courses, or four if salad is included, in the dining room.

CAVIAR TORTE

4 eggs, hard-cooked and chopped
2 tablespoons mayonnaise
2 tablespoons plain yogurt
1 teaspoon Dijon-style mustard
3 green onions, chopped
8 ounces cream cheese
1/4 cup sour cream
Dash of Tabasco sauce
1 jar (2 ounces) Icelandic caviar
Parsley sprigs
Crisp flatbread or sesame crackers

Mix together the eggs, mayonnaise, yogurt, and mustard and spread in a straight-sided glass bowl, 6 to 8 inches in diameter. Sprinkle with green onions. Beat cream cheese with sour cream and Tabasco sauce until creamy and spread over the onions. Top with caviar, cover and chill. To serve, circle bowl with parsley sprigs and pass with crackers. Makes 8 servings.

TOMATO SOUP WITH CHIVES

1 tablespoon butter
2 large yellow onions, chopped
2 cans (6 ounces each) tomato paste
6 cups chicken stock
2 garlic cloves, minced
2 whole cloves
4 tomatoes, peeled and quartered
3/4 teaspoon crumbled dried basil
3 tablespoons chopped parsley
1/2 teaspoon salt
1/2 teaspoon freshly ground black pepper
1/4 cup sour cream or plain yogurt
1 tablespoon chopped chives

In a large saucepan melt the butter and sauté the yellow onions until golden. Add the tomato paste, stock, garlic, and cloves, stir well, cover, and simmer for 25 minutes. Let cool slightly. Turn into a food processor or blender container and add tomatoes, basil, half the parsley, salt, and pepper. Blend until smooth. Return puréed mixture to the saucepan and heat through. Serve in bowls topped with sour cream or yogurt, the remaining parsley, and chives. Makes 8 servings.

TIVOLI CHICKEN AND HAM ROLLS

8 large split chicken breasts
8 slices smoked ham (about 4 ounces)
8 slices samsoe or fontina cheese (about 4 ounces)
3 tablespoons dry fine bread crumbs
1/4 teaspoon salt
1/4 teaspoon freshly ground black pepper
3 tablespoons grated Romano cheese
1 egg, beaten
3 tablespoons butter
1/4 cup chicken stock
1/3 cup dry vermouth

Bone and skin chicken breasts. Lay each chicken breast out flat and pound lightly between 2 sheets of waxed paper to achieve an equal thickness. Cover each chicken breast with a slice of ham and one of cheese. Roll up and fasten with toothpicks. Combine the bread crumbs, salt, pepper, and Romano cheese. Dip rolled breasts in egg and then in bread-crumb mixture. In a large skillet melt butter and brown chicken rolls, turning to brown all sides. Transfer rolls to a baking dish. Pour stock and vermouth into skillet placed over medium heat and deglaze pan. Pour stock mixture over chicken rolls. If desired, refrigerate at this point until ready to finish cooking. Bake in a 350° F. oven, un-covered, until meat is white clear to the center, about 20 to 30 minutes. Makes 8 servings.

GLAZED CARROTS

6 to 8 large carrots, peeled and sliced on the diagonal
2 tablespoons butter
1 tablespoon Dijon-style mustard
1 tablespoon firmly packed brown sugar
1/2 teaspoon freshly ground black pepper
Dash of salt

Cook carrots in a small amount of boiling salted water in a covered saucepan until tender, about 8 minutes; drain well. Add to carrots in saucepan butter, mustard, sugar, pepper, and salt and stir gently to blend carrots and seasonings. Cook over medium heat until carrots are glazed. Makes 8 servings.

CHOCOLATE–GLAZED MARZIPAN TORTE

1-1/2 cups almonds
1-3/4 cups powdered sugar
5 egg whites
1/8 teaspoon salt
1/8 teaspoon cream of tartar
Chocolate Butter Cream (following)

Grind almonds in a blender or food processor until a fine powder. Add powdered sugar and process together. In a large bowl beat egg whites until foamy, add salt and cream of tartar, and beat until stiff, glossy peaks form. Gently fold nut mixture into the egg whites. Spread in a buttered and floured 9-inch spring-form pan. Bake in a 350° F. oven for 30 minutes, or until golden brown. Let cool on a wire rack. Spread top of cake with Chocolate Butter Cream swirled in a design. Cut in wedges to serve. Makes 12 servings.

CHOCOLATE BUTTER CREAM In the top pan of a double boiler melt 4 ounces semi-sweet chocolate over hot water; let cool. Beat 4 tablespoons (1/4 cup) butter, at room temperature, until creamy, and mix in 1/2 cup powdered sugar and 1/2 teaspoon vanilla extract. Stir in melted choco-late and blend well. Makes about 1 cup.

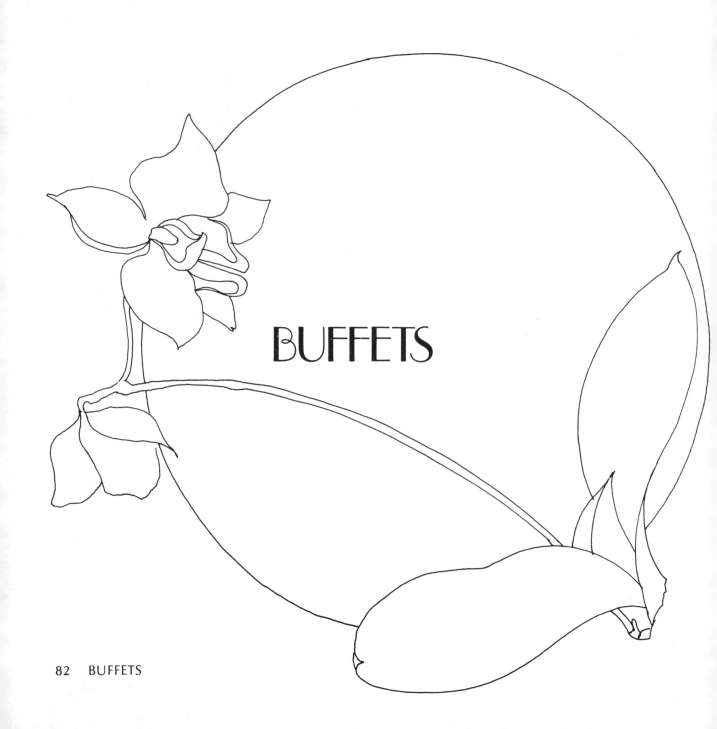

BUFFETS

Indisputably, buffets are the most serene way to entertain a large number of guests. The fare can be imaginative and avant-garde despite the fact it must sit and linger on the table.

Zero in on a provocative ethnic theme. A Nordic seafood sampling, a Viennese appetizer party, a French country buffet, or an Aegean mezé spread each capture a gay mood. Other celebrations may revolve around a pastry-wrapped meat loaf or a cold gingered pork roast, served with unusual salads and spectacular desserts.

Easy-to-eat finger or fork fare is a prime criterion of the menu. These buffets also have the asset of make-ahead preparations to leave the host or hostess unharried on the party day.

SERVES TWELVE PERSONS

Steak Strips Garni
Ham and Sunflower Squares
Sausage and Mushroom Triangles
Endive with Shrimp
Marinated Artichoke Hearts (optional)
Specialty Breads: Dark Rye, Brioche, and Salt Sticks
Wine: Tasting of Sauvignon Blancs and Cabernet Sauvignons
Coffee Bar: Filtered Coffee Plus Condiments

This gracious Continental party features an array of easy-to-serve hot and cold appetizers with a sideboard offering specially brewed coffee, whipped cream, and liqueurs. The combination makes for an aesthetic buffet supper for a dozen or more.

SHOPPING LIST Purchase the ingredients for the special recipes, plus 2 jars (6 ounces *each*) marinated artichoke hearts, if serving, and a selection of breads to accompany the meal.

COOK AHEAD Assemble the Sausage and Mushroom Triangles up to two weeks ahead and freeze unbaked. Thaw before baking. Or assemble a day or two in advance and refrigerate. Bake the ham squares a day in advance and reheat. Prepare the steak the morning of the party. The other components go together swiftly.

SERVING LOGISTICS Set up the appetizer buffet on one table or a buffet sideboard and arrange the coffee bar at another station. Print a special menu on a blackboard or card suggesting coffee combinations for special drinks.

Viennese Appetizer Party

STEAK STRIPS GARNI

2- to 2-1/2-pound top sirloin
    steak
1/4 teaspoon salt
1/2 teaspoon freshly ground
    black pepper
2 tablespoons olive oil
1 shallot, chopped
1 garlic clove, minced
1/3 cup dry red wine
1/3 cup beef stock
1/2 teaspoon freshly grated
    lemon peel
1/2 cup sour cream
1/2 cup plain yogurt
1 jar (4 ounces) red or black
    caviar
1/3 cup finely chopped chives
    or green onions
1/3 cup finely chopped
    parsley

Season the meat with salt and
pepper and brown in oil in a
large skillet, turning to brown
both sides through to the
medium-rare stage. Transfer to
a platter. Add the shallot,
garlic, wine, and stock to the
drippings and cook down until
reduced by half. Stir in lemon
peel. Slice meat in thin strips
and arrange slices, overlapping
them, on a platter. Pour over
sauce. Mix together sour cream
and yogurt and spoon in a
ribbon down the center. Spoon
caviar in a strip down the
center of sour-cream ribbon
and sprinkle chives or green
onions and parsley along either
side. Chill until ready to serve.
Makes 12 to 16 appetizer
servings.

HAM AND SUNFLOWER SQUARES

12 eggs
1-1/2 cups sour cream
1-1/2 teaspoons salt
1/2 pound cooked ham, cut
    in julienne strips
1/2 cup finely chopped
    parsley
1/2 cup finely chopped
    green onions
8 ounces Swiss cheese,
    shredded (2 cups)
1/2 cup roasted sunflower
    seeds
2 tablespoons butter, melted

Beat eggs until blended and
mix in sour cream, salt, ham,
parsley, onions, cheese, and
half the seeds. Pour into a
well-buttered 10- by 15-inch
jelly roll pan. Sprinkle with
remaining seeds and drizzle
with melted butter. Bake in a
350° F. oven for 25 to 30
minutes, or just until set. Cut
in small squares and serve
hot. (If desired, bake in
advance and reheat in a 350°
F. oven for 15 to 20 minutes,
or until hot through.) Makes
about 48 squares.

SAUSAGE AND MUSHROOM TRIANGLES

1 pound mild Italian sausages
2 green onions, chopped
5 tablespoons butter
1/2 pound mushrooms,
    chopped
1/4 cup dry fine bread crumbs
1 egg, beaten
4 ounces Swiss cheese,
    shredded (1 cup)
About 8 sheets fila dough

Place sausages in a saucepan, add water to cover, cover pan, bring to a boil, and remove from heat. Let stand for 15 minutes. Drain, remove skins from sausages, and chop. Transfer sausage to a mixing bowl. Meanwhile, in a large skillet sauté onions in 2 tablespoons of the butter until glazed. Add mushrooms and sauté 1 minute. Remove from heat and place in the mixing bowl with the chopped sausage, along with the crumbs, egg, and cheese. Mix lightly. Melt remaining 3 tablespoons butter. Lay out 1 sheet of fila dough (keep remaining sheets covered with plastic wrap so they won't dry out) and lightly brush with melted butter. Cut crosswise into 3-inch-wide strips. Place a rounded teaspoon of filling at narrow end of each strip and fold over one corner. Continue folding from side to side like a flag,

making a triangle shape. Place on a lightly buttered baking sheet. Proceed in this manner with remaining fila and filling. Brush tops of triangles with melted butter. (If desired, freeze at this point, tightly covered. Let thaw at room temperature before baking.) Bake in a 375° F. oven for 15 minutes, or until golden brown. Serve hot. Makes about 48 triangles.

ENDIVE WITH SHRIMP

3 bunches Belgian endive
1/3 cup Curry- flavored Mayonnaise (following)
1/3 pound cooked small shrimp
2 cups cherry tomatoes

Separate endive into individual leaves and spread a little mayonnaise at the tip of each. Place 2 shrimp on top. Mound the cherry tomatoes in the center of the platter and surround with endive, tips pointing outward. Makes about 24 appetizers.

CURRY-FLAVORED MAYONNAISE
Sauté 1 teaspoon curry powder in 1 teaspoon butter in a small saucepan for 2 minutes to rid the powder of the raw taste. Let cool and stir into 1/3 cup mayonnaise.

COFFEE BAR

Brew a specially ground and roasted coffee for the occasion, using a filter-style coffee maker. If possible, make espresso as well. Set out the coffee with cups or heatproof glasses. Arrange alongside a bowl of whipped cream, shredded or grated semisweet chocolate, cinnamon sticks, slivered orange peel, and freshly grated nutmeg. Include several liqueurs and after-dinner liquors, such as Grand Marnier or Cointreau, Cognac, Armagnac, rum, and Kahlúa.

SERVES TWENTY PERSONS

Hummus and Taramasalata with Lahvosh
Keftethes (Parsley Meatballs)
Dolmathes   Mushrooms   Cherry Tomatoes
Feta Cheese   Greek Olives   Pistachios to Shell
Spinach Pitas   Shrimp Pitas
Grapes
Halvah and Baklava
Wine: Retsina, Tavel Rosé, or California Red

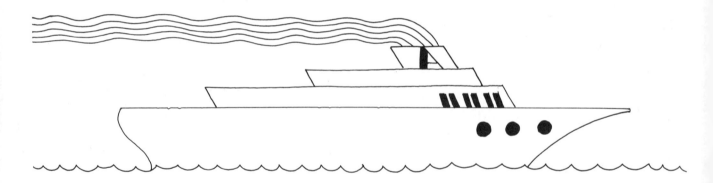

The carefree nature of an Aegean appetizer buffet agilely lends itself to entertaining a crowd with ease. The Greeks, with their zest for good living, have a well-developed custom of socializing with wine and mezé, meaning a little something to whet the appetite. Mezé in various degrees of complexity are always offered at the convivial tavernas and at family holiday gatherings. As the spontaneous dancing and conversation continue, the appetizers can easily become the meal.

This party idea captures the merriment of a mezé party. The plan is to handle twenty guests for an appetizer through dessert buffet. The foods are authentically Greek, with a nod or two to the Turks. The dishes all sit well without diminishing in flavor. Middle Eastern specialty markets or delicatessens carry many of the necessities. Go there for fila (paper-thin dough), feta, olives, canned dolmathes, tarama (carp roe), tahini (ground sesame seeds), and lahvosh (bubbly Armenian cracker bread). You may also purchase baklava and halvah, the sesame-seed candy.

To complement the food, serve retsina or carafes of red wine and have Greek music playing on the stereo in the background.

SHOPPING LIST In addition to the ingredients needed for the special recipes, plan to buy 1 large can dolmathes, mushrooms, cherry tomatoes, 1 pound feta cheese, 1 quart Greek olives, 1 pound pistachio nuts in the shell, 3 pounds seedless grapes, 1 pound halvah, and baklava.

COOK AHEAD Two or three weeks in advance assemble and freeze the pitas, if desired, making one recipe of each. Three or four days in advance make two recipes each of Hummus (page 50) and Taramasalata. The meatballs are best made one or two days ahead and refrigerated. They can, however, be made in advance and frozen.

SERVING LOGISTICS Set out the appetizers on a buffet table preferably in the garden or on the patio and let guests help themselves.

TARAMASALATA

2 slices white bread, crusts
   removed
1 jar (4 ounces) tarama (carp
   roe)
1/4 cup fresh lemon juice
1/4 cup chopped green
   onions
1/3 cup olive oil
1/3 cup salad oil
Minced parsley
Lahvosh or thinly sliced
   cucumber

Dip bread in water to moisten,
then press out any excess
moisture. Place in the container
of a blender or food processor
the bread, tarama, lemon juice,
and onions and blend or
process until smooth. Gradually pour in the oils, blending
until thick and creamy. Pour
into a bowl and chill. To
serve, mound in a bowl and
sprinkle with parsley. Surround
with lahvosh or sliced cucumbers for spreading tarama
mixture on. Makes about 1-
1/2 cups.

KEFTETHES
(Parsley Meatballs)

2 large onions, finely chopped
1 tablespoon olive oil
1 tablespoon butter
2 cups soft white bread
   crumbs
1 cup water
4 eggs
4 garlic cloves, minced
1 tablespoon salt
2 teaspoons crumbled dried
   oregano
1/2 cup finely chopped fresh
   parsley
2 tablespoons chopped fresh
   mint (optional)
2 pounds lean ground lamb
2 pounds ground turkey
1/2 cup red-wine vinegar
Freshly ground black pepper
Dried oregano leaves

In a large skillet sauté the
onions in oil and butter until
golden brown; turn into a
large mixing bowl. Add bread
crumbs, water, eggs, garlic,
salt, oregano, parsley, and
mint, if desired, and mix well.
Add ground meats and mix
thoroughly. Shape into balls
about 1 inch in diameter and
place 1 inch apart on a lightly
greased baking pan. Bake in a
425° F. oven for 20 minutes,
or until cooked through. In a
small saucepan boil the vinegar
until reduced by half, add
pan drippings from the baked
meatballs and heat until
blended. Place meatballs in a
serving dish, and pour the
sauce over them. Grind pepper
over and sprinkle with
crumbled dried oregano. Makes
about 72.

SPINACH PITAS

1 bunch (about 6) green
   onions, finely chopped
1 tablespoon olive oil
1 large bunch spinach,
   trimmed and finely chopped
8 ounces cream cheese, at
   room temperature
5-1/2 ounces feta cheese
2 eggs
1/2 cup freshly grated
   Parmesan cheese
1/4 teaspoon freshly ground
   black pepper
1/4 cup finely chopped
   parsley
1/8 teaspoon ground nutmeg
8 ounces fila dough
1/4 pound (1/2 cup) butter,
   melted

In a large skillet sauté the onions in oil until limp. Add spinach and cook over medium-high heat just until barely wilted, about 2 minutes. Remove from heat and let cool. Beat together the cream cheese, feta cheese, eggs, Parmesan, and pepper. Mix in parsley, nutmeg, and sautéed vegetables.

Lay out 1 sheet of fila dough (keep remaining fila sheets covered with plastic wrap so they won't dry out) and lightly brush with melted butter. Cut crosswise into 3-inch-wide strips. Place a rounded teaspoon of spinach-cheese filling on narrow end of each strip and fold over one corner to form a triangle. Continue folding from side to side like a flag, making a triangle shape. Place on a lightly buttered baking sheet. Proceed in this manner with remaining fila and filling. Brush tops of triangles with melted butter. (If desired, freeze at this point, tightly covered. Let thaw at room temperature before baking.) Bake in a 350° F. oven for 15 minutes, or until golden brown. Serve hot. Makes about 72 triangles.

SHRIMP PITAS

8 ounces cream cheese, at room temperature
1 egg
1/4 cup finely chopped parsley
2 green onions, finely chopped
1 teaspoon fresh lemon juice
1 teaspoon freshly grated lemon peel
Dash of Worcestershire sauce
1/4 teaspoon salt
1/2 pound cooked small shrimp or chopped cooked crab or lobster meat
1/3 cup freshly grated Parmesan cheese
About 8 sheets fila dough
6 tablespoons sweet (unsalted) or clarified butter, melted

Beat cream cheese until creamy and mix in egg, parsley, onions, lemon juice and peel, Worcestershire sauce, salt, shrimp, crab, or lobster, and Parmesan. Mix just until evenly distributed. Lay out 1 sheet of fila dough (keep remaining sheets covered with plastic wrap so they won't dry out) and lightly brush with melted butter. Cut crosswise into 3-inch-wide strips. Place a rounded teaspoon of cheese filling on narrow end of each strip and fold over one corner. Continue folding pastry from side to side like a flag, making a triangle shape. Place on a lightly buttered baking sheet. Proceed in this manner with remaining fila and filling. Brush tops of triangles with melted butter. (If desired, freeze at this point, tightly covered. Let thaw at room temperature before baking.) Bake in a 350° F. oven for 15 minutes, or until golden brown. Serve hot. Makes about 48 triangles.

SERVES SIXTEEN PERSONS

Nosegay of Crudités with Tapenade
Pistachio-studded Chicken Terrine
Pork and Veal Terrine with Hazelnuts
Chicken Liver Pâté in Brioche
Cheese Tray: Brie, Roquefort, Gruyère, and Chèvre
French Bread and Sweet Butter
Basket of Nectarines and Grapes
Wines: Johannisberg Riesling, Zinfandel,
Muscadet, Burgundy, and/or French Sauternes

This easy-going cold buffet is splended for various types of parties and any size group. It suits a wedding reception, surprise birthday, open-house buffet, or a charity party. Its great virtue is its make-ahead ease. In addition, the pâtés may be purchased to streamline the preparation even further. This party plan is detailed for sixteen guests. It is easily multiplied to handle a crowd of forty.

SHOPPING LIST In addition to the ingredients for the special recipes, buy 3 loaves sweet French bread, 1 pound sweet butter, 1/2 pound each brie, Roquefort or blue, and chèvre, 1 pound Gruyère or Jarlsberg, and 3 pounds nectarines and 2 pounds grapes. If desired, instead of making the terrines and pâté, purchase 4 pounds of two or three kinds of terrines and/or pâtés.

COOK AHEAD Three or four days in advance of the party make the Pistachio-studded Chicken Terrine and the Pork and Veal Terrine with Hazelnuts. Two days ahead of time prepare a double batch of Tapenade and blend the Chicken Liver Pâté. The day of the party encase the pâté in the brioche, arrange the vegetables in a large wicker basket, and set out the fruits and cheeses.

SERVING LOGISTICS Set up the menu buffet style so that guess are free to return for additional tasting as often as they wish.

French Country Buffet

NOSEGAY OF CRUDITES

Purchase a selection of about eight kinds of vegetables, such as button mushrooms, radishes, zucchini, cherry tomatoes, carrots, pea pods or sugar peas, jicama, cauliflower, red or green peppers, fennel, celery, and cucumbers. Cut into pieces suitable for dipping. Place a flower frog in a wicker basket and nestle the vegetables in the basket, tucking parsley or Romaine leaves between them. Accompany with bowls of Tapenade, following.

TAPENADE

2 egg yolks
1-1/2 tablespoons fresh lemon juice
1-1/2 tablespoons white-wine vinegar
3/4 teaspoon salt
1/2 teaspoon sugar
2 teaspoons Dijon-style mustard
1 cup safflower oil
1 garlic clove, minced
2 tablespoons chopped capers
2 tablespoons chopped parsley
2 tablespoons chopped chives
1 teaspoon grated lemon peel
4 anchovy fillets, finely chopped

Place in a blender container the egg yolks, lemon juice, vinegar, salt, sugar, and mustard. Blend a few seconds. With motor running, gradually pour in oil in a fine, steady stream. Blend in garlic. Stir in capers, parsley, chives, lemon peel, and anchovy fillets. Turn into a refrigerator container. Cover and chill until serving time. Spoon into a bowl or stoneware crock to serve. Makes about 1-1/4 cups.

PISTACHIO–STUDDED CHICKEN TERRINE

1 tablespoon butter
1 large onion, finely chopped
3 tablespoons dry sherry
3 large split chicken breasts (totaling about 1 pound), boned and skinned
1-1/4 pounds lean ground pork
2 eggs
2 teaspoons salt
1 teaspoon freshly grated lemon peel
3/4 teaspoon ground allspice
1/2 teaspoon freshly ground black pepper
2 garlic cloves, minced
1/4 cup rich, gelatinized chicken stock
1/3 cup powdered nonfat dry milk
6 tablespoons pistachios
2 small bay leaves
6 pink or black peppercorns

In a medium skillet melt butter and sauté onion until translucent. Pour in sherry to deglaze pan. Place chicken in a food processor fitted with a steel blade and grind until finely minced. (Or grind in a food grinder.) Add to the food processor container the onions and sherry, pork, eggs, salt, lemon peel, allspice, ground pepper, garlic, chicken stock, and milk powder. Process just until lightly mixed, a few seconds. (Or mix in a mixing bowl.) Spread half the mixture in a greased 9- by 5-inch loaf pan. Sprinkle with half the pistachios. Cover with remaining meat mixture and sprinkle with remaining nuts. Decorate with bay leaves and pink or black peppercorns, making a design in the center. Cover with foil, place in a pan containing 1 inch hot water, and bake in a 350° F. oven for 1-1/2 hours or until cooked through. Remove from water bath and chill loaf at least 1 day, or up to 4 days. Turn out on a platter and slice to serve. Makes 16 appetizer servings.

PORK AND VEAL TERRINE WITH HAZELNUTS

2 tablespoons butter
1/4 cup chopped shallots or green onions (white part only)
1/4 pound mushrooms, sliced
1/2 pound chicken livers
1 teaspoon dried thyme
1/2 teaspoon ground allspice
1/2 teaspoon white pepper
3 tablespoons brandy or Cognac
1/4 cup dry vermouth
1 pound ground pork
1 pound ground veal
2 eggs, beaten
2 teaspoons salt
1/3 cup broken hazelnuts or Brazil nuts

In a large skillet melt 1 tablespoon of the butter and sauté shallots or green onions and mushrooms for 2 minutes; turn out of pan into a bowl. Add remaining butter to skillet and sauté chicken livers with thyme, allspice, and pepper until livers are nicely browned but still pink inside. Pour in brandy or Cognac and turn out of pan into the bowl with mushrooms. Deglaze pan with vermouth and pour the drippings into the bowl. Process the mushroom-liver mixture in a food processor fitted with a steel blade or a blender. Turn into a large mixing bowl. Add pork, veal, eggs, and salt and mix just until well blended. Reserve a few nuts to garnish the top and mix in remainder. Pat into a greased 9- by 5-inch loaf pan. Scatter remaining nuts over the top. Cover with foil, place in a pan containing 1 inch water, and bake in a 350° F. oven for 1-1/2 hours. Remove from water bath and chill loaf at least 1 day, or up to 4 days. Turn out on a platter and slice to serve. Makes 16 appetizer servings.

CHICKEN LIVER PATE IN BRIOCHE

1 round loaf Brioche
  (following)
6 ounces (3/4 cup) butter
1 pound chicken livers
1/4 pound mushrooms,
  chopped
3 green onions (white part
  only), chopped
3 tablespoons chopped
  parsley
1/2 teaspoon crumbled dried
  thyme
1/2 teaspoon salt
1/4 teaspoon freshly ground
  black pepper
2 tablespoons brandy or
  Cognac
1/4 cup dry white vermouth
  or wine
Butter for Brioche

Prepare the Brioche. In a large skillet, melt 2 tablespoons of the butter and sauté chicken livers with mushrooms, green onions, parsley, thyme, salt, and pepper, stirring often, until livers are firm but still slightly pink inside. Add brandy or Cognac and cook down slightly. Remove livers and mushrooms from pan with a slotted spoon. Add wine and deglaze pan, reducing juices by half. Pour reduced juices over livers and let cool to room temperature. Purée in a food processor or blender. Beat remaining butter until creamy and mix in the liver purée, mixing until smoothly blended. If desired, prepare in advance to this point, cover, and refrigerate.

To serve, slice off the top 3/4 inch of the Brioche loaf, making a cap, and set aside. With a long, slender serrated bread knife, cut out the inside of the loaf in this manner: Cut around the inside of the loaf 1/2 inch in from the outside, cutting to within 1/2 inch of the bottom. Then cut in from the bottom 1/2 inch and swing the knife in an arc to release the inside cut cylinder of the loaf. Pull out this center section of the loaf and reserve. Spread the hollowed out interior of the loaf lightly with butter, then spoon in the pâté, mounding it attractively on top. Wrap and chill. At serving time cut the reserved center part of the loaf into thin slices. Place the pâté-stuffed Brioche on a plate and encircle with the sliced Brioche. Let guests spread their own pâté. Makes 16 servings.

BRIOCHE Prepare the dough for French Brioche Braid (page 123). Let dough rise until doubled in size, punch down, and turn out on a lightly floured board. Divide in half, shape into 2 balls and place each ball in a greased 1-pound coffee can. Cover and let rise until double (dough will almost fill can). Bake in a 350° F. oven for 30 minutes, or until loaf sounds hollow when thumped. Let cool 5 minutes, then remove from cans. Loaves should shake out with ease. Makes 2 loaves. (Use 1 loaf for pâté recipe and reserve second loaf for another use.)

SERVES SIXTEEN PERSONS

Gravlax with Mustard-Dill Sauce
Pickled Halibut and Shrimp
Herring in Sour Cream
Tiny Oysters on the Half Shell (optional)
Caviar and Sour Cream
Assorted Breads: Rye, Pumpernickel, and Brioche
Sweet Butter
Aquavit (optional)   Champagne

Scandinavian Seafood Party

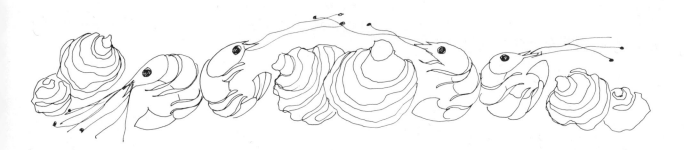

This alluring appetizer buffet featuring chilled and pickled seafood is dazzling and festive for any season. Prepare it completely in advance so you may present it good-naturedly at the last minute. The menu works equally well as an elegant appetizer or supper party. To transpose the menu to a complete meal, present a cheese and fruit tray and a platter of assorted Danish butter cookies.

SHOPPING LIST For a party for sixteen guests, buy the ingredients for the special recipes, plus the following: 2 jars (6 ounces each) herring in sour cream, 8 ounces caviar, and, if desired, 1 pound tiny Olympia oysters. For breads, purchase 1 large loaf dark rye bread, 1 loaf thinly sliced pumpernickel, and 1 large loaf thinly sliced brioche bread. Have sweet butter on hand.

COOK AHEAD The pickled salmon and halibut are best prepared two days in advance. The other elements go together swiftly.

An attractive way to serve the aquavit is to encase it in a block of ice. It is easy to achieve by placing the bottle of liqueur in an empty milk carton and filling the carton with water up to the bottle neck. Then store in the freezer for one day. After the water is frozen, simply peel off the carton and the bottle is sealed in a block of ice.

SERVING LOGISTICS Set out the seafood on the buffet table, ready for the guests to help themselves. Arrange the sliced breads in a basket or on a board. The ice block of aquavit should be placed on a tray to catch the water drips. Nest the champagne in an iced tub.

GRAVLAX WITH MUSTARD–DILL SAUCE

2-1/2-pound salmon fillet, with skin removed (one side of fish)
2 tablespoons salt
1/4 cup sugar
2 tablespoons brandy or Cognac
12 black peppercorns
2 tablespoons finely chopped fresh dill, or 1 teaspoon crumbled dried dill
Buttered brioche slices
Mustard-Dill Sauce (following)

Place the salmon fillet in a shallow baking dish. Mix together the salt, sugar, brandy or Cognac, peppercorns, and dill and spoon over the fish. Cover tightly with clear plastic wrap and chill 2 days, basting several times with the accumulating juices.

To serve, drain off juices and place fish on a board.

Slice very thinly on the diagonal. For serving, overlap salmon slices on buttered bread and spoon over the Mustard-Dill Sauce. Makes about 16 appetizer or first-course servings.

MUSTARD-DILL SAUCE Beat 1 egg yolk in a small bowl with a wire whisk until well blended, then beat in 2 tablespoons Dijon-style mustard, 4 teaspoons sugar, 1-1/2 tablespoons white-wine vinegar, 2 teaspoons fresh lemon juice, 1/2 teaspoon salt, 1-1/2 teaspoons finely chopped fresh dill or 1/4 teaspoon crumbled dried dill, and a dash of white pepper. Gradually whisk in 1/3 cup safflower oil.

PICKLED HALIBUT AND SHRIMP

2-pound chunk halibut
1/2 pound large shrimp
3 slices lemon
1 teaspoon salt
1 bay leaf
1 teaspoon whole mixed
  pickling spices
1 small sweet onion, sliced
  and separated into rings
2/3 cup white-wine vinegar
1/2 cup dry white wine
1/3 cup sugar

Place the halibut and shrimp in a large saucepan and cover with water. Combine lemon slices, salt, bay leaf, and pickling spices in a cheesecloth bag or place in a tea ball and add to pan. Cover, bring to a boil, and simmer for 8 to 10 minutes, or until fish barely flakes with a fork. Drain off stock and let fish cool. Remove skin and bones. Break fish along its natural seams into 1- to 2-inch chunks. Peel and devein shrimp. Alternate fish, shrimp, and onion rings in a 1-1/2-quart jar or crock. Combine vinegar, wine, and sugar in a saucepan. Bring to a boil and simmer, stirring, until sugar dissolves. Pour into jar with halibut and shrimp so that fish is covered with liquid. Cover and chill for 1 or 2 days to allow flavors to permeate. Makes 16 appetizer servings.

NOTE Fresh mussels are excellent poached and pickled in this same fashion, letting them replace both the halibut and shrimp. Time their cooking to 5 to 6 minutes, or just until the shells open and the mussels turn a bright coral color.

CAVIAR AND SOUR CREAM

Set out your favorite caviar with side bowls of sour cream and minced sweet onion or chopped chives, letting guests compose their own canapes.

SERVES TWELVE PERSONS

Vichyssoise
Veal and Sausage Loaf en Croûte with Chive Sauce
Green Salad with Condiments
Hot Buttered French Brioche Braid or French Bread
Cheese Tray: St. André and Chèvre
Strawberry and Grand Marnier Bombe with Berries
Wine: Champagne, Chenin Blanc, or Chardonnay, and Pinot Noir
Coffee

This refined party buffet is designed for a celebration: a wedding, anniversary, or simply a dinner with good friends. Though outlined here for a dozen, it is easy to prepare for twice the number.

SHOPPING LIST Purchase the ingredients for the special recipes, plus 8 ounces *each* of St. André and chèvre cheese and the bread, if it is not to be home baked.

COOK AHEAD Make the Vichyssoise a day or two ahead and refrigerate. Assemble the veal loaf a day ahead of time, ready for final baking at party time, or freeze well in advance. The bombe is quick to create in advance and freeze. Bake two loaves of French Brioche Braid (page 123) ahead and freeze (or buy the bread). Make the Shallot Dressing two or three days ahead and refrigerate.

SERVING LOGISTICS Pass the soup, served in chilled cups or frosty glasses, as a "walk-around" first course. Set up the buffet table with the sliced veal loaf, chive sauce, salad with bowls of condiments, and hot buttered bread. Later offer the bombe and coffee.

VICHYSSOISE

2 tablespoons butter
4 leeks, thinly sliced (white part only)
1 large onion, chopped
5 medium potatoes, peeled and sliced
4 cups chicken stock
1/2 teaspoon salt
3/4 teaspoon crumbled dried tarragon
1/2 teaspoon freshly ground black pepper
2 cups milk
1 cup whipping cream
1/4 cup dry sherry
Finely chopped chives

In a large soup kettle or saucepot melt butter and sauté leeks and onion until barely golden. Add potatoes, stock, salt, tarragon, and pepper and simmer for 30 minutes. Let cool slightly. Purée in a blender or food processor. Stir in milk and chill. When cold, add cream and sherry and adjust seasoning. To serve, ladle into 12 large-bowled wine goblets, cups, or mugs and sprinkle with chopped chives. Makes 12 servings.

Gala Garden Buffet

VEAL AND SAUSAGE LOAF EN CROUTE

3/4 pound mild Italian
  sausages (about 3 sausages)
1 tablespoon butter
2 medium onions, finely
  chopped
1-1/2 pounds ground veal or
  turkey
1 pound lean ground pork
1/2 pound bulk pork sausage
4 garlic cloves, minced
3 tablespoons dry sherry
2 teaspoons salt
1 teaspoon crumbled dried
  thyme
1 teaspoon ground allspice
1/2 teaspoon freshly ground
  black pepper
2 tablespoons finely chopped
  parsley
4 eggs, lightly beaten
1/2 cup soft French-bread
  crumbs
4 ounces Jarlsberg or Swiss
  cheese, shredded (1 cup)
1/2 cup nonfat dry milk
  powder
Cream Cheese Pastry
  (following)
Egg wash: 1 egg yolk, beaten
  with 2 tablespoons milk
Chive Sauce (following)

Place sausages in a saucepan, add water to cover, cover pan, bring to a boil, and remove from heat. Let stand for 15 minutes; drain and let cool. In a medium skillet melt butter and sauté onions until golden. Turn into a mixing bowl along with the ground meats, garlic, sherry, salt, thyme, allspice, pepper, parsley, eggs, crumbs, cheese, and powdered milk and mix just until blended.

Line up sausages end to end down the center of a greased baking pan at least 14 inches long. Pat meat mixture over, around, and under sausages, encasing them in the center of the mixture and making a 4- by 14-inch log. Chill 15 minutes to firm up. Bake in a 375° F. oven for 30 minutes. Let cool, then chill.

On a lightly floured board roll out pastry into a rectangle about 10 by 18 inches. Place meat roll on it, top side down, and bring up dough to encase roll, pinching edges together to seal. Trim off any scraps of pastry and place

roll, seam side down, on a greased baking sheet. Reroll scraps and make cutouts with a cookie cutter, using a star or scalloped pattern, and arrange on top. If desired, cover and refrigerate 1 day. Brush with egg wash. Bake in a 425° F. oven for 30 minutes, or until golden brown. Serve hot or cold, cut in slices. Accompany with Chive Sauce. Makes 12 to 14 servings.

CREAM CHEESE PASTRY Place in a mixing bowl 8 ounces cream cheese, at room temperature, and 1/2 pound (1 cup) butter, at room temperature, and beat until creamy. Beat in 1/4 cup whipping cream. Gradually add 2-1/2 cups all-purpose flour and 1/2 teaspoon salt and mix until dough forms a ball. Pat together and chill briefly.

CHIVE SAUCE Stir together 1 cup sour cream, 1/2 cup plain yogurt, 1/4 teaspoon freshly ground black pepper, and 3 tablespoons *each* chopped chives and chopped parsley. Refrigerate until ready to serve. Makes about 1-1/2 cups.

GREEN SALAD WITH CONDIMENTS

1 large head Romaine lettuce
2 large heads butter lettuce
Shallot Dressing (following)

CONDIMENTS
1 can (7-1/2 ounces) roasted
   sunflower seeds
4 hard-cooked egg yolks,
   shredded
1/4 pound bacon, cooked
   until crisp and crumbled
3 avocados, diced
8 ounces alfalfa sprouts

Tear greens into bite-size pieces and store in a large plastic bag in the refrigerator. To serve, place greens in a large salad bowl and pour over just enough dressing to coat. Surround with bowls of condiments to spoon over. Makes 12 servings.

SHALLOT DRESSING Place in a blender container 1-1/3 cups safflower oil, 1/2 cup red-wine vinegar, 1-1/2 teaspoons salt, 1/4 teaspoon freshly ground black pepper, 2 table-spoons Dijon-style mustard, and 3 shallots or white part of green onions or 2 garlic cloves. Blend, pour into a tall, slender bottle, cover, and chill. Shake well before using. Makes about 2 cups.

STRAWBERRY AND GRAND MARNIER BOMBE

1-1/2 quarts strawberry ice
   or raspberry sherbet
1 cup plus 2 teaspoons sugar
1/3 cup water
6 egg yolks
2 teaspoons freshly grated
   orange peel
2 cups whipping cream
1/4 cup Grand Marnier
4 cups strawberries, hulled

Pack strawberry ice or rasp-berry sherbet firmly into the bottom and sides of a 2-1/2-quart ice cream or salad mold, making an even layer about 3/4 inch thick. Freeze until firm.

Combine 1 cup sugar and water in a small saucepan and bring to a boil, stirring to dissolve sugar. Boil until temperature registers 238° F. on a candy thermometer (soft-ball stage). Meanwhile, beat egg yolks until thick and pale yellow. Continuing to beat yolks, slowly pour in the sugar syrup in a fine, steady stream. Beat until mixture cools to room temperature, about 7 minutes, then cover and chill until cold. Mash orange peel with 2 teaspoons sugar to bring out its oils; stir into yolk mixture. Whip cream until stiff and beat in Grand Marnier. Fold in yolk mixture. Spoon into the center of the ice-lined mold, filling to the top. Cover and freeze until firm.

To serve, dip mold in a pan of hot water a few seconds, then invert on a serving platter. Pass strawberries in a bowl alongside. Cut bombe in wedges to serve. Makes 12 servings.

SERVES FORTY PERSONS

Smoked Turkey   Baked Ham
Assorted Mustards   Red Pepper Jelly   Cranberry Chutney
Assorted Breads: Buttered Rolls, Rye, Egg Twist
Natural Cream Cheese   Jarlsberg Cheese
Crudités: Cherry Tomatoes, Jícama, Alfalfa Sprouts, Zucchini
Layered Guacamole Dip
Baskets of Apples, Pears, and Grapes
Hot Glögg   Sparkling Apple Juice

It's a Holiday Family Party

The holiday season is a festive time to invite families of all ages for an open-house supper. In my neighborhood it has become a Christmas Eve tradition to gather at one home. This party plan works well for a company buffet luncheon as well, since cooking tasks are minimal.

SHOPPING LIST For forty guests, buy a 15-pound ready-to-serve ham and an 18- to 20-pound already-smoked turkey, or else purchase an uncooked ham and turkey and plan to cook them. Purchase 2 pounds natural cream cheese and a 4- or 5-pound wedge of Jarlsberg cheese, 1 quart cherry tomatoes, 1 pound alfalfa sprouts, 1 pound zucchini, and 1 large jícama. Count on 2 dozen apples and pears combined, plus 2 or 3 pounds of seedless red flame grapes. Also buy assorted breads and mustards and the ingredients for the special recipes.

COOK AHEAD If the turkey is not already smoked, plan to smoke-barbecue it in a covered barbecue a day or two ahead. If the ham is not ready-to-serve, bake and glaze it ahead as well. Purchase the jelly or preserve it in season. Make the chutney several days ahead. Mix the Layered Guacamole Dip (page 20) a few hours ahead and imbed the pit in it to prevent it from darkening.

SERVING LOGISTICS Set out the menu as a buffet table in the dining room or kitchen or utilize both. Guests may create their own open-face sandwiches as finger food, or if preferred provide small paper plates and forks. Various sandwich combinations are possible with the array of ingredients.

SMOKED TURKEY

Season an 18- to 20-pound turkey with salt and pepper and rub it both inside and out with several minced garlic cloves. Place the turkey on a foil pan and insert a meat thermometer in the thickest part of a thigh. Ignite about 30 briquets in a barbecue with a cover and let them burn down. Place turkey on the barbecue and cook over fairly low heat (about 325° F.), covered, until a meat thermometer reaches about 175° F. Allow 3-1/2 to 4 hours. Let cool and chill. Slice thinly to serve.

RED PEPPER JELLY

6 large red bell peppers, halved and seeded
2 tablespoons salt
1-1/2 cups white or apple cider vinegar
6 cups sugar
1 bottle (7 ounces) liquid pectin

Finely chop the peppers in a food processor or by hand. Turn into a large bowl, sprinkle with salt, and let stand 30 minutes. Drain and rinse under cold water. Place peppers in a large saucepot and add vinegar and sugar. Bring to a boil and add the pectin. Boil until jelly is thick and "sheets" when dropped from a spoon, about 20 minutes. Pour into hot sterilized jars and seal. Process in boiling water bath for 10 minutes. Makes about 4 half-pints.

CRANBERRY CHUTNEY

1 pound cranberries
2 cups sugar
Zest of 1 orange, slivered
1 orange, peeled, sectioned, and diced
2 golden delicious apples, cored and diced
1/2 cup apple-cider vinegar
1 teaspoon finely chopped peeled ginger root
1 stick cinnamon
1/4 teaspoon dried hot red chili peppers
1/4 cup chopped pecans or walnuts

Place all ingredients in a large saucepot. Bring to a boil, stirring. Reduce heat to simmer and cook, uncovered, until thickened, about 20 minutes. Ladle into jars, cover, and refrigerate. Makes about 4 half-pints.

HOT GLOGG

8 oranges
Whole cloves
2 cups rum
2 gallons apple cider
6 sticks cinnamon

Stud oranges with 8 to 10 cloves each. Place in a baking pan and bake in a 300° F. oven for 2 hours, or until juices start to run. Transfer to a heatproof 2-1/2- to 3-quart serving container, such as a large metal bowl or copper pan. Warm the rum and pour it over the oranges, reserving about 1 tablespoon. Ignite the tablespoon of rum, add to oranges and rum and let flame. Heat apple cider and pour in. Add cinnamon sticks. Makes about forty-eight 6-ounce servings.

Ethnic Celebration Buffet

This party buffet dovetails specialties from several cuisines for an eye-catching summer meal. Vivid colors and lively flavors keynote the spread. A pyramid of cracked wheat forms the salad, pistachios stud the pork roast, vibrant eggplant, tomatoes, and peppers create the one hot dish, and dessert is a cone of flavored cheese with raspberry sauce cascading down its sides. Select it for a celebration: an anniversary, a wedding supper, or a toasting party.

SERVES SIXTEEN PERSONS

Spinach Pitas (optional)
Ham and Sunflower Squares (optional)
Tabbouleh
Gingered Pork with Pistachios
Ratatouille
Cheese Romanoff with Raspberry Sauce and Berries
Wine: Champagne, Tasting of Zinfandels or Cabernet Sauvignons
Coffee   Iced Tea

SHOPPING LIST Purchase the ingredients for the special recipes.

COOK AHEAD Roast the meat two days in advance and chill. Slice early on the day of the party and refrigerate. Both the Tabbouleh and the Cheese Romanoff may be prepared two days ahead of time. Arrange them on platters several hours in advance. Let the Ratatouille be the one hot dish, although in very warm weather, plan to cook it in advance and serve it chilled. If appetizers are desired, serve Spinach Pitas (page 90) and Ham and Sunflower Squares (page 86).

SERVING LOGISTICS Commence the party with champagne and appetizers, if desired. Then proceed to the buffet table.

TABBOULEH

3 cups cracked wheat (bulgur)
About 6 cups water
2 large bunches parsley, stems removed
2 large bunches (12 to 14) green onions, cut in 1-inch lengths
3/4 cup fresh mint leaves
1 cup olive oil
1/2 cup fresh lemon juice
2 teaspoons salt
2 teaspoons ground allspice
1/2 teaspoon freshly ground black pepper
2 heads Romaine lettuce
1 pint cherry tomatoes
2 lemons, cut in wedges
1/2 pint Mediterranean-style olives
About 8 mint sprigs
3 jars (6 ounces each) marinated artichoke hearts (optional)

Place cracked wheat in a large bowl, pour over water, and let stand 1 hour, or until puffed. (If necessary, add additional water.) Drain thoroughly. In a food processor fitted with a steel blade process the parsley, onions, and mint leaves a few seconds, just until finely chopped, doing about 2 cupfuls at a time. (Or use a blender.) Turn out of the container into the puffed wheat. Mix together the olive oil, lemon juice, salt, allspice, and pepper. Pour over the wheat mixture and mix lightly. Cover and chill, up to 2 days.

Just before serving, line 3 or 4 large platters with the inner leaves of the Romaine, tips pointing outward. Mound the cracked wheat mixture in the center in a pyramid and encircle with cherry tomatoes, lemon wedges, olives, mint sprigs, and marinated artichoke hearts, if desired. Makes 16 servings.

GINGERED PORK WITH PISTACHIOS

6-pound loin of pork, boned
3 garlic cloves, slivered
2 teaspoons green peppercorns
1/4 cup pistachios
1/4 cup golden raisins
4 tablespoons Dijon-style mustard
2 tablespoons soy sauce
2 teaspoons chopped peeled ginger root
1/2 teaspoon ground allspice
Watercress or parsley sprigs
Candied kumquats or pickled sweet red peppers

Lay out the meat flat on a board and sprinkle with half the garlic, the peppercorns, pistachios, and raisins. Roll up and tie with a string. Mix together mustard, soy sauce, ginger root, allspice, and re- maining garlic and spread over the surface of the roast. Place on a roasting pan, insert a meat thermometer, and roast in a 325° F. oven until ther- mometer registers 175° F., about 2 hours. Remove meat to a platter and chill. To serve, slice thinly and arrange on a platter. Garnish with watercress or parsley sprigs and kumquats or peppers, each of the latter cut to resemble a flower. Makes about 16 servings.

RATATOUILLE

2 large eggplants
Salt
About 1/3 cup olive oil
2 large onions, thinly sliced
6 garlic cloves, minced
4 large zucchini, thinly sliced

1 red bell pepper, seeded
   and cut in pieces
1 green bell pepper, seeded
   and cut in pieces
6 medium tomatoes, peeled
   and diced
1 teaspoon salt
1/2 teaspoon freshly ground
   black pepper
4 teaspoons chopped fresh
   basil, or 1 teaspoon
   crumbled dried basil
1/3 cup minced parsley

Cut eggplants in half length- wise, then cut into 1-1/2- to 2-inch pieces. Sprinkle with salt and let stand 10 minutes for juices to exude; rinse off salt and pat dry. In a large skillet or Dutch oven heat 1/4 cup of the oil and sauté onions until limp. Add garlic, zucchini, and red and green peppers and sauté for a few minutes longer. Add eggplant to the sautéed vegetables and drizzle over remaining oil. Mix in tomatoes and season with salt, black pepper, and basil. Cover and bake in a 350° F. oven for 1-1/2 hours, or until vegetables are cooked through. Turn into a serving casserole and sprinkle with parsley. Makes 16 servings.

CHEESE ROMANOFF WITH RASPBERRY SAUCE

1-1/2 pounds natural cream
   cheese, at room temperature
6 egg yolks
3/4 cup sugar
3 tablespoons Cognac or
   brandy, or 1 tablespoon
   vanilla extract
3 tablespoons whipping cream
Raspberry Sauce (following)
6 cups strawberries, hulled

Place in a food processor fitted with a steel blade the cheese, egg yolks, sugar, Cognac, brandy, or vanilla extract, and cream. Process just until blended, a few seconds. Line a charlotte mold or other mold with cheese- cloth and spoon in cheese. Cover and chill overnight.

   To serve, unmold and pour over Raspberry Sauce. Accom- pany with leaf-lined baskets of strawberries. Makes 16 servings.

RASPBERRY SAUCE Thaw 2 pack- ages (10 ounces *each*) frozen raspberries. Purée in a blender and then press through a wire sieve, discarding seeds.

SPECIALTY
PARTIES

Surprise and frivolity make a great party. What better way to ensure a party's success than to let the guests participate? Here they get involved in such preparations as cranking ice cream or assembling pizzas, or they fill their own pocket-bread sandwiches, match cheese and fruit combinations, blind-taste wines, or sample soups and chocolate treats.

These fun-filled activities automatically entertain the guests and lighten the demands on the host or hostess. Plus they make for big parties with small price tags.

SERVES TWENTY–FOUR PERSONS

Norwegian Jarlsberg with Golden Delicious Apples
Danish Havarti with Red Peppers
Danish or Oregon Blue Cheese with Fennel
Dutch Leyden with Cucumbers
Port Salut with Pears
Provolone with Pineapple
Brie with Grapes
St. André with Peaches or Nectarines
Bandon Cheddar or Candian Black Diamond Cheddar
with Red Delicious Apples
Chèvre or Natural Cream Cheese with Mushrooms
Baguettes, English Wafers, and Sweet Butter
Wine: Tasting of Zinfandels and Sauvignon Blancs

Almost-Instant Cheese-Tasting Party

For an almost-spur-of-the-moment party that requires no cooking, consider a cheese-tasting buffet, mating each cheese with a complementary fruit or vegetable. This is appropriate for any season. In the autumn the red peppers, fennel, and apples are at their prime to feature. In summer, the stone fruits can shine. Wine goes splendidly with the cheese tasting. A tasting of zinfandels and sauvignon blancs from various wine makers would be a natural. Or simply set up carafes of red and white table wine if the budget is limited. Offer a combination of at least six cheeses paired with a fruit or vegetable from the menu selections.

SHOPPING LIST Figure on four ounces of cheese per person. Cheese keeps well so it is best to buy a generous amount and count on using the balance in other ways. Figure on one and a half whole fruits and a lesser amount of vegetables per person. For example, offer a combination of three cheeses and fruits and three cheeses and vegetables for two dozen guests and plan on one dozen apples, one dozen pears, and two whole pineapples.

COOK AHEAD None is required.

SERVING LOGISTICS Serve buffet style, with suggested cheese and vegetable or fruit combinations set out in clusters. The cheese should be on boards, ready for slicing. Apples and pears should have a special fruit cutter alongside that effortlessly removes the core and cuts the fruit in wedges. The pineapple should be cut in cubes or spears, the stone fruits set out with a small knife, the grapes piled in a basket with scissors alongside for snipping into individual bunches, and the vegetables precut into pieces suitable as finger food. Slice the baguettes and pile in a basket with the wafers. Spoon the sweet butter into a crock.

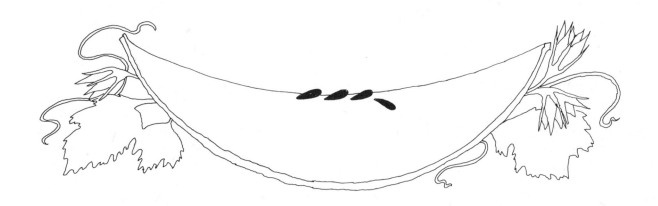

SERVES EIGHT PERSONS

The Farmer's Vegetable Soup
Cheese Tray: Gruyère and Monterey Jack
Sweet French Bread, Crusty Rolls, or Bread Sticks
Wine: Tasting of Zinfandels, Cabernet Sauvignons, or Sauvignon Blancs
Fruit Basket of the Season

An informal wine-tasting event gains more appeal when a light soup supper is presented simultaneously. This peasant-style leek and potato soup resolves the dilemma of providing a savory, nourishing soup that does not detract from the tasting. For this party plan, the host should select eight different bottles of wine: perhaps all California zinfandels, cabernet sauvignons, sauvignon blancs, or chenin blancs of a current year. It is quite proper to split the costs of the wine among the guests, so everyone shares in the expenses.

SHOPPING LIST Buy the ingredients for the soup recipe, plus a generous amount of bread and cheese: 2 loaves of French bread and 2 pounds of cheese. Purchase a selection of seasonal fruits, such as pears, apples, and grapes, or summer's stone fruits.

COOK AHEAD The soup is easily made a day in advance.

SERVING LOGISTICS The wines should be opened at the proper advance time for breathing, individually bagged in brown bags, and then either numbered or lettered. Each guest should be seated at the table, with a setting of eight wineglasses. It is appropriate to have them bring their own glasses.

THE FARMER'S VEGETABLE SOUP

2 tablespoons butter
1 large onion, finely chopped
2 bunches leeks, sliced
2 quarts rich chicken stock
3 medium potatoes
2 teaspoons chopped fresh tarragon, or 1/2 teaspoon crumbled dried tarragon
Salt and freshly ground black pepper to taste
1/4 cup finely chopped parsley
2 cups (1 pint) whipping cream
4 ounces grated Gruyère or fontina cheese, grated (1 cup)

In a large saucepot, melt butter and sauté onion and leeks until glazed. Add stock, **potatoes**, tarragon, salt and **pepper and** cover and simmer **for 15** minutes, or until **tender**. Purée in a food processor or mash with a potato masher. Ladle into soup bowls and sprinkle with parsley. Pass a pitcher of cream and a bowl of cheese for guests to add as desired. Makes 8 servings.

Blind Wine-Tasting Party

During the holidays a soup-supper open house makes a casual change from the typical cocktail buffet. The concept is special because all ages, from toddlers to great-grandmas, are included. Strangers and neighbors meet and become friends as they break bread around an informal table. With two substantial full-meal soups, homemade breads, and cheese and fruit, the spread suits a five to eight supper gathering. This menu is geared for a crowd of two to three dozen drop-in guests.

SERVES THIRTY–SIX PERSONS

Veal-Barley Soup
Greek Lentil Soup
Assorted Breads: Dark Rye, Whole Wheat, French
Assorted Cheeses: Norwegian Jarlsberg,
Canadian Black Diamond
Cheddar, Asiago, Dry Monterey Jack
Fruit Basket: Pears, Red and Golden Delicious Apples,
Red Flame and Muscat Grapes
Wine: Carafes of Red and White Table

Open House for Soup

SHOPPING LIST In addition to the ingredients needed for the soups, plan to buy 4 loaves of bread and 4 pounds of assorted cheeses for three dozen guests, or make the bread if you have the time. Allow one piece of fruit per person.

COOK AHEAD Both soups are easily made two days in advance. Purchase the breads or bake one or two kinds in advance and freeze.

SERVING LOGISTICS Serve the soups in the kitchen if desired, in handsome containers placed on warmers, in crockpots, or big kettles placed directly on the range. Plan to ladle into mugs for easier handling. Arrange the cheeses and breads so guests may help themselves. Set out fruit in baskets with an apple cutter for simplicity. Seat the guests in turn at the table. If the crowd becomes too many for the chairs, let guests wait their turn with a glass of wine.

GREEK LENTIL SOUP

3 onions, finely chopped
3 stalks celery, finely chopped
3 carrots, peeled and chopped
1/3 cup olive oil
4-1/2 cups lentils
2 bay leaves
4 garlic cloves, minced
1-1/2 teaspoons salt
1/2 teaspoon freshly ground
    black pepper
6 quarts water
1 can (6 ounces) tomato paste
1/2 cup red-wine vinegar
1-1/2 teaspoons crumbled
    dried oregano

In a large soup kettle sauté onions, celery, and carrots in oil until limp. Add the lentils, bay leaves, garlic, salt, pepper, and water. Cover and simmer until lentils are tender, about 1 to 1-1/2 hours. Add the tomato paste, vinegar, and oregano and simmer 30 minutes longer. Makes 24 servings.

VEAL–BARLEY SOUP

5 pounds meaty veal shanks
3 onions, finely chopped
3 tablespoons olive oil
6 quarts water
6 beef bouillon cubes
1/2 teaspoon freshly ground
    black pepper
3 carrots, peeled and diced
3 stalks celery, finely chopped
2 cups barley
2 cans (15 ounces *each*) stewed
    tomatoes

In a large soup kettle brown veal shanks and onions in oil. Add water, bouillon cubes, and pepper, bring to a boil, cover, and simmer for 1-1/2 to 2 hours, or until meat is tender. Remove veal shanks and skim fat off broth. Remove meat from bones and dice meat. Bring broth to a boil and add carrots, celery, and barley. Cover and simmer for 1 hour, or until barley is tender. Add meat and tomatoes and heat through. Taste for seasoning. Makes about 24 servings.

SERVES TWENTY–FOUR PERSONS

Pocket Bread with Greek Meat Sauce
Assorted Condiments
Hummus with Lahvosh
Skewered Cherry Tomatoes, Mushrooms, and Olives
Yogurt Almond Cake
Fruit Basket
Sparkling Apple Juice or Jug Red Wine

Greek Pocket Bread Buffet

Making one's own pocket-bread sandwiches is especially fun for a teenage gathering. This informal Mediterranean party suits various occasions throughout the day: a midday lunch, swim party, or late afternoon or evening supper. The major cooking revolves around simmering a spicy meat sauce and baking decorative cakes. Happily these may both be made and frozen up to a month in advance.

SHOPPING LIST Purchase the ingredients for the special recipes, plus 3 dozen pocket (pita) breads (allowing 1 dozen extra). For condiments, buy 3 cans (7-1/2 ounces *each*) roasted sunflower seeds, 3 bunches green onions, 1-1/2 pounds Monterey jack cheese, 1 pint yogurt, 1 pint sour cream, and 2 heads iceberg lettuce. For skewered relishes, buy 2 cans (15-1/2 ounces *each*) large pitted ripe olives, 2 quarts cherry tomatoes, and 2 pounds button mushrooms. Also purchase 1 bag lahvosh (bubbly Armenian cracker bread), or sufficient sesame crackers to accompany the Hummus, and a selection of seasonal fruits: grapes, strawberries, or apples. Figure on three servings to each bottle of sparkling apple juice or a half bottle of wine per person.

COOK AHEAD Prepare the meat sauce and bake two cakes a day or two in advance or up to a month ahead and freeze. Prepare two recipes Hummus (page 50) up to three days in advance and refrigerate. (Any leftover Hummus may be frozen for future use.)

SERVING LOGISTICS Set up the party buffet style, planning on two separate food set-ups or lines. Keep meat sauce warm in crockpots or electric saucepots. Cut pocket breads in half and arrange in baskets. Prepare condiments for stuffing into pocket bread with meat sauce and place in separate bowls. Thread relishes on short bamboo skewers. Mound Hummus in a serving bowl and surround with lahvosh or sesame crackers. Set out the cakes already sliced and offer the fruit in a leaf-lined basket.

GREEK MEAT SAUCE

6 large onions, chopped
6 pounds lean ground beef,
    or 3 pounds *each* lean ground
    beef or lamb and turkey
1 tablespoon whole mixed
    pickling spices
8 garlic cloves, minced
6 cans (6 ounces *each*) tomato
    paste
4 teaspoons salt
1 teaspoon ground cumin
1 teaspoon ground allspice
1 teaspoon freshly ground
    black pepper
1/4 cup red-wine vinegar

Place in a large saucepot the
onions, meat, pickling spices
(tied in a cheesecloth bag or
placed in a tea ball), garlic,
tomato paste, salt, cumin, allspice, pepper, and vinegar.
Cover and simmer very slowly,
stirring occasionally to keep
meat crumbly, for 3 hours, or
until thickened. Skim off any
extra fat. Makes about 4-1/2
quarts, or enough for 24 servings.

FREEZER TIP When cooled to
room temperature, ladle into
freezer containers or plastic-
coated ice cream containers,
cover, and freeze.

YOGURT ALMOND CAKE

1/2 pound (1 cup) butter or
    margarine, at room
    temperature
1-1/2 cups sugar
4 eggs
1 teaspoon freshly grated
    orange peel
1 teaspoon vanilla extract
1 cup plain yogurt
2-1/2 cups all-purpose flour
1 teaspoon baking powder
1 teaspoon baking soda
3/4 cup finely chopped
    almonds or walnuts

In a large mixing bowl beat
butter until creamy and gradually beat in sugar. Add eggs,
one at a time, and beat after
each addition until smooth. Mix
in orange peel, vanilla extract,
and yogurt. Stir together the
flour, baking powder, and baking
soda and add to the creamed
mixture, beating until incorporated. Mix in the nuts. Turn
into a buttered and floured 10-
inch plain or fluted tube pan.
Bake in a 350° F. oven for 1
hour, or until a toothpick inserted
in the center comes out clean.
Place on a rack and let cool 10
minutes. Turn out of pan and
let cool completely on a rack.
Makes 12 to 14 servings; bake
2 cakes for a gathering of 24
persons.

International Bread, Cheese & Fruit Party

SERVES THIRTY PERSONS

Greek Christopsomo, Natural Cream Cheese, and Strawberries
French Brioche Braid, Gruyère or Norwegian Jarlsberg Cheese,
Thinly Sliced Ham, and Pears
Walnut Bread, Blue, Brie, or St. André Cheese, and Grapes
Orange Rye Bread, Canadian or Oregon Cheddar, and Golden Delicious Apples
Danish Almond Twist, Sweet Butter, and Fresh Pineapple Cubes
Kir

This walk-about garden party is a splendid way to entertain any number of guests in an imaginative style. Arrange an artful combination of ethnic breads, cheeses, and fruits at four different stations and let guests help themselves. The food itself is so decorative that the centerpieces may be minimal. Tiny baskets of assorted field flowers or a few floating blossoms— begonias or camelias—look pretty. Kir, the French aperitif blending an imported crème de cassis liqueur or syrup and a dry white wine, makes a delightful, easy-to-pour beverage.

SHOPPING LIST If time is at a premium, purchase the breads instead of baking them. For example consider Portuguese sweet bread as a substitute for the Greek Christopsomo, let dark rye loaves replace the Walnut Bread, and have light rye or pumpernickel stand in for the Orange Rye Bread. Offer at least four different breads, making the sweet yeast bread, such as Danish Almond Twist, optional. Figure on at least three ounces of cheese per person, but it's best to be generous as cheese keeps well. For a party of thirty guests, buy 2 pounds natural cream cheese, 3 pounds Gruyère cheese, 2 pounds blue cheese, and 3 pounds Cheddar cheese, plus 1 pound of thinly sliced ham.

Also purchase 3 gallons dry white wine and 1 fifth imported crème de cassis or cassis syrup. For fruits, buy 1 dozen apples, 1 dozen pears, 3 pounds grapes, 3 baskets straw-berries, and 2 pineapples.

COOK AHEAD Plan to bake the breads two to three weeks in advance and freeze them, or substitute ones from a good bakery.

SERVING LOGISTICS Have four or five stations or tables available so that each combination of bread, cheese, and fruit may be clustered together. Set out the Greek Christop-somo bread whole, then slice it as needed by cutting it into thirds and then in slices. Plan to thinly slice the other breads, butter them, and reassemble them in a loaf shape. Wrap in foil and reheat in a 350° F. oven for 15 to 20 minutes, or until hot through, just before serving.

Arrange the cheeses on boards, ready for slicing. Serve apples and pears with a special fruit cutter alongside. (This cutter automatically cuts the fruit in one motion, removing the core and slicing the fruit into wedges.) Mound the grapes in a wicker or wire basket with scissors alongside for easy snipping off of a bunch. Pile the berries (prefer-ably big ones with stems still on) in a leaf-lined basket ready for eating out of hand. March a row of berries down the top of the log of natural cream cheese for a pretty touch. Halve the pineapples lengthwise, cut the pulp away from the shells, cut it into cubes, and serve the cubes in the pineapple halves.

Serve the Kir in a glass pitcher to pour directly into wineglasses.

FRENCH BRIOCHE BRAID

1 package (1 tablespoon)
  active dry yeast
1/4 cup lukewarm water
1/4 pound (1/2 cup) butter,
  at room temperature
2 tablespoons sugar
1 teaspoon salt
3 eggs
1/2 cup lukewarm milk
3-1/4 cups all-purpose flour

Sprinkle yeast into warm water, stir to dissolve, and let stand until foamy, about 10 minutes. In a large mixing bowl beat butter, sugar, salt, and eggs together and stir in milk. Add 1 cup flour and beat until smooth. Mix in the yeast mixture. Gradually add remaining flour, adding only enough to make a soft dough. Turn out on a lightly floured board and knead until smooth and satiny. Place in a greased bowl, butter top lightly, cover, and let rise in a warm place until doubled in bulk, about 1-1/2 hours.

  Punch down dough, turn out on a lightly floured board, and knead lightly. Cut into 3 pieces and roll out each piece between the palms of the hands into a rope about 22 inches long. Overlap strips at one end and braid into a long braid, tucking in the ends. Place diagonally on a large buttered baking sheet. Cover and let rise in a warm place until doubled in size. Bake in a 325° F. oven for 35 minutes, or until golden brown. Let cool on a wire rack. Makes 1 large braided loaf.

ORANGE RYE BREAD

2-1/2 cups water
1 cup quick-cooking oatmeal
2 packages (1 tablespoon
  each) active dry yeast
2-1/2 teaspoons salt
1 orange
1/3 cup (5-1/3 tablespoons)
  butter
1/4 cup molasses
1 cup milk
1-1/2 cups whole-wheat flour
1 cup rye flour
3 cups all-purpose flour

Place in a saucepan 2 cups of the water and the oatmeal; bring to a boil, boil 1 minute, and turn into a mixing bowl; let cool to lukewarm. Sprinkle yeast into the remaining 1/2 cup lukewarm water, stir to dissolve, and let stand until foamy, about 10 minutes. With a vegetable peeler, remove zest from orange in strips and chop finely. Add to the oatmeal mixture the yeast, salt, orange peel, butter, and molasses. Heat milk until lukewarm and stir in. Gradually add the whole-wheat, rye, and all-purpose flours, mixing to make a soft dough. Turn out dough on a lightly floured board and knead until smooth and satiny. Place in a bowl, butter top lightly, cover, and let rise until doubled in bulk, about 1-1/2 hours.

  Punch down dough, turn out on a lightly floured board, and knead to remove bubbles. Divide into 3 parts and shape each into a loaf. Place in buttered 9- by 5-inch loaf pans or shape into round loaves and place on buttered baking sheets. Cover and let rise until doubled in size, about 45 minutes. Bake in a 375° F. oven for 35 to 40 minutes, or until the loaves sound hollow when thumped. Let cool on a wire rack. Makes 3 loaves.

WALNUT BREAD

1 package (1 tablespoon)
   active dry yeast
1/4 cup lukewarm water
3/4 cup milk
3 tablespoons butter
3 tablespoons sugar
1 teaspoon salt
1 egg
About 3 cups all-purpose flour
3/4 cup broken walnut
   halves, lightly toasted
1 egg white, lightly beaten

Sprinkle yeast into lukewarm water, stir to dissolve, and let stand until foamy, about 10 minutes. Scald milk and pour over butter and sugar in a large mixing bowl; let cool to lukewarm. Stir in salt, egg, and yeast mixture. Gradually add flour, beating well and adding only enough to make a soft dough. Mix in the nuts. Turn out on a lightly floured board and knead until smooth and satiny. Place in a greased bowl, butter top lightly, cover, and let rise until doubled in bulk, about 1-1/2 hours.

Punch down dough, turn out on a lightly floured board, and knead lightly. Shape into a flat cake. Place in a buttered 9-inch round cake pan. Cover and let rise until doubled in size. Brush with beaten egg white. Bake in a 350° F. oven for 35 to 40 minutes, or until loaf sounds hollow when thumped. Let cool on a wire rack. Makes 1 loaf.

GREEK CHRISTOPSOMO
(Greek Christmas Bread)

2 packages (1 tablespoon
   each) active dry yeast
1/2 cup lukewarm water
1/2 cup milk
6 ounces (3/4 cup) butter
1/2 cup sugar
4 eggs
2 teaspoons aniseed,
   crushed
1 teaspoon salt
5 cups all-purpose flour
9 walnut halves
1 egg white, lightly beaten

Sprinkle yeast into warm water, stir to dissolve, and let stand until foamy, about 10 minutes. Heat milk and butter together until butter melts. Pour into a mixing bowl, add sugar, and let cool to lukewarm. Add eggs, one at a time, and beat after each addition until smooth. Mix in yeast mixture, aniseed, salt, and 2 cups of the flour, and beat at medium speed for 5 minutes. Gradually add remaining flour, using a heavy-duty electric mixer or wooden spoon.

Turn out dough on a lightly floured board and knead until smooth and satiny, about 10 minutes. Place dough in a bowl, butter top lightly, cover, and let rise in a warm place until doubled in bulk, about 1-1/2 hours.

Punch down dough, turn out on a lightly floured board, and knead lightly. Pinch off 2 pieces of dough, each about 3 inches in diameter. Shape remaining ball of dough into a smooth flat cake, about 9 inches in diameter, and place on a greased baking sheet. Roll each of the small balls into a 14-inch rope and cut a 5-inch slash in the end of each. Cross ropes on the center of the round loaf. Curl slashed sections away from center, forming a small circle, and place a walnut half in each circle and one in the center of the cross. Cover and let rise until almost doubled in size, about 1 hour.

Brush loaf with egg white. Bake in a 325° F. oven for 50 to 55 minutes, or until golden brown and the loaf sounds hollow when thumped. Serve hot or let cool on a wire rack. To serve, cut in thirds, then cut in 1- to 2-inch-thick slices. Makes 1 large loaf.

DANISH ALMOND TWIST

1 package (1 tablespoon) active dry yeast
1/4 cup lukewarm water
1/4 pound (1/2 cup) butter, at room temperature
1/3 cup sugar
1/2 teaspoon salt
2 teaspoons vanilla extract
3 eggs
3-3/4 cups all-purpose flour
3/4 cup lukewarm milk
Almond or Chocolate Streusel Filling (following)
1 egg white, lightly beaten
Sugar
Sliced almonds

Sprinkle yeast into lukewarm water, stir to dissolve, and let stand until foamy, about 10 minutes. In a large mixing bowl beat butter until creamy and beat in sugar, salt, vanilla extract, and eggs. Add 1 cup of the flour and beat well.

Add the yeast mixture and milk and beat until smooth. Gradually add remaining flour, beating until smooth with a heavy-duty electric mixer or wooden spoon. Turn out on a lightly floured board and knead until smooth and satiny. Place in a greased bowl, butter top lightly, cover, and let rise until doubled in bulk, about 1-1/2 hours.

Punch down dough, turn out on a lightly floured board, and knead lightly. Cut dough in half. Roll out one-half into a 10- by 14-inch rectangle. Spread with half of filling of choice. Roll up from long side and place seam side down on a buttered baking sheet. Repeat with other half of dough and remaining filling. Cut through roll to within 1/2 inch of the bottom at 3/4-inch intervals and pull and twist each slice to lay flat on baking sheet, laying the first slice to the left side, the second to the right, and continuing to alternate sides to the end of the roll. Cover and let rise until doubled in size, about 45 minutes. Brush loaves with egg white and sprinkle with sugar and almonds. Bake in a 350° F. oven for 25 to 30

minutes, or until golden brown. Let cool on wire racks. Makes 2 loaves.

ALMOND FILLING Mix together 1 can (8 ounces) almond paste, 4 tablespoons (1/4 cup) butter, at room temperature, 1/3 cup finely chopped almonds, and 1 egg, beating until smooth and well blended.

CHOCOLATE STREUSEL FILLING Mix until crumbly 1/2 cup sugar, 1/4 cup all-purpose flour, 2 tablespoons butter, 4 teaspoons unsweetened cocoa powder, and 1/2 teaspoon ground cinnamon.

KIR

For thirty persons, purchase 3 gallons dry white wine and 1 fifth imported crème de cassis or cassis syrup. Chill the wine and the crème de cassis or cassis syrup. Pour off of each gallon of wine 1-1/4 cups of wine and replace it with 1-1/4 cups cassis liqueur or syrup. This produces a delicate, rose-colored semisweet drink. The French prefer a richer ratio of cassis to wine, but a lighter blend is favored in the States.

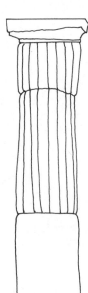

SERVES TWELVE PERSONS

Trio of Pizzas
Romaine Salad
Amaretto Strawberry Bombe or Assorted Gelati
Lemonade, Beer, Chianti, or Gamay Beaujolais Nouveau

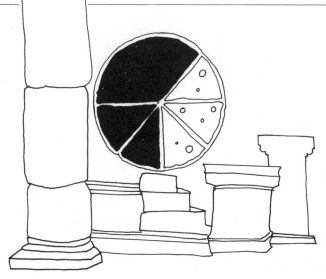

In this participation-style party, call upon the guests to assemble the pizzas while the host provides the basic dough. It makes for a frolicsome party, particularly for a young crowd. This repertoire of three different pizzas should serve a dozen guests, but any leftover pizza freezes well. Select the beverage to suit the crowd.

SHOPPING LIST Purchase the ingredients for the special recipes, plus lettuce. If the party is a spontaneous, last-minute affair, substitute commercial gelati (Italian ice creams) for the bombe.

COOK AHEAD Make the bombe at least a day in advance or up to two weeks ahead of time and freeze, covered. Plan to mix the pizza dough an hour before the guests arrive. Have the ingredients ready for topping the pizzas. Mix a favorite green salad at the last minute.

SERVING LOGISTICS Set out the pizzas buffet style, cut in wedges so guests may sample each kind, along with the salad. Follow with the dessert course.

Pizza-Making Party

TRIO OF PIZZAS

1 package (1 tablespoon)
  active dry yeast
1 tablespoon sugar
1-3/4 cups lukewarm water
1-1/2 teaspoons salt
3 tablespoons safflower or
  olive oil
About 5 cups unbleached or
  all-purpose flour,
  or 2-1/2 cups *each*
  unbleached and whole-
  wheat flour
Salami and Cheese Topping
  (following)
Beef and Mushroom Topping
  (following)
Sausage and Ricotta Topping
  (following)

Sprinkle yeast and sugar into warm water in a large mixing bowl. Stir to dissolve and let stand until foamy, about 10 minutes. Add salt and oil and gradually add 2 cups of the flour, beating until smooth. Gradually add remaining flour, adding only enough to make a soft dough. Turn out on a lightly floured board and knead until smooth and no longer sticky. Cover with plastic wrap and let stand for 15 minutes, or up to 1 hour. Divide dough in 3 equal pieces. Place each piece on an oiled 14-inch pizza pan or a 10- by 15-inch baking pan. With oiled finger-tips press dough into pan, covering it completely. Cover each pan of dough with one of the following fillings. Bake in a 450° F. oven for 20 minutes, or until golden brown on the edges. Makes 3 large pizzas, or enough for about 12 servings.

SALAMI AND CHEESE TOPPING
Onto the dough-lined pizza pan spread 1 can (8 ounces) tomato sauce and sprinkle with 1 teaspoon crumbled dried oregano. Cover with 18 slices Italian dry salami, 3 green onions, chopped, 1/2 cup sliced ripe olives, and 6 ounces Monterey jack cheese, shredded (1-1/2 cups). Sprinkle with 1/3 cup grated Parmesan or Romano cheese. Makes enough topping for 1 pizza.

BEEF AND MUSHROOM TOPPING
In a large skillet sauté 1/2 pound mushrooms, thinly sliced, in 2 tablespoons butter just until limp. Mix in 3 green onions, chopped. Spread dough-lined pizza pan with 1 can (8 ounces) tomato sauce and sprinkle with 1 teaspoon crumbled dried oregano. Cover with sautéed mushrooms and onions and crumble over 1 pound lean ground beef, pork, or turkey. Sprinkle with 6 ounces Monterey jack cheese, shredded (1-1/2 cups), and 1/3 cup grated Parmesan or Romano cheese. Makes enough topping for 1 pizza.

SAUSAGE AND RICOTTA TOPPING

Place 1 pound mild Italian sausages in a saucepan, add water to cover, cover, bring to a boil, and remove from heat. Let stand for 15 minutes. Drain and slice sausage thinly. In a mixing bowl beat 4 eggs until light and beat in 1 pound (1 pint) ricotta cheese. Mix in 1/4 cup grated Parmesan cheese, 2 green onions, chopped, 1/4 cup chopped parsley, and the sliced sausage. Spoon into a dough-lined pizza pan and cover with 6 ounces Mozzarella cheese, sliced, and 1/4 cup grated Parmesan or Romano cheese. Makes enough topping for 1 pizza.

AMARETTO STRAWBERRY BOMBE

1 quart strawberry or raspberry sherbet
3/4 cup crumbled almond
   macaroons (amaretti)
1/4 cup amaretto liqueur
   (optional)
1 cup whipping cream
1/4 teaspoon almond extract
   (omit if using liqueur)
1-1/2 pints vanilla ice cream,
   slightly softened
1/2 cup toasted chopped
   blanched almonds
1/3 cup coarsely grated
   semisweet chocolate
Strawberries or raspberries

Pack sherbet into a 2-1/2-quart ice-cream mold (or salad or pudding mold) and freeze until firm. Sprinkle macaroon crumbs with 2 tablespoons of the liqueur, if desired. Whip cream until stiff and beat in remaining liqueur, if desired, or almond extract. In a chilled bowl beat ice cream until it is light and forms mounds. Quickly fold in whipped cream, almonds, chocolate, and macaroon crumbs. Turn into sherbet-lined mold. Cover and freeze until firm. To serve, dip mold into hot water for a few seconds, then invert onto a serving platter. Ring with berries. Makes 12 servings.

SERVES SIXTEEN PERSONS

Chocolate Grand Marnier Torte
Chocolate-glazed Raspberry Torte
Chocolate-sheathed Rum Praline Cake
Coffee and Liqueurs

Indulging in elegant chocolate-flavored desserts has great party appeal on rare occasions. So why not transform the party scene into a fashionable Viennese pastry shop? These three gala chocolate cakes have almonds, Grand Marnier, and raspberries for accent. As a dessert party, each cake serves sixteen, letting guests sample one or all.

SHOPPING LIST Purchase the ingredients for the specialty cakes.

COOK AHEAD Make the cakes a day or two in advance or two or three weeks ahead of time and freeze them. Or to simplify preparations, ask two of the guests to each bring a cake.

SERVING LOGISTICS Set out the pastries buffet style and slice thinly so guests are free to sample each kind. Offer coffee and, if desired, a choice of liqueurs.

Viennese Konditorei Party for Chocolate Lovers

CHOCOLATE GRAND MARNIER TORTE

6 ounces semisweet chocolate
2 cups finely ground almonds
2 tablespoons all-purpose flour
1/4 pound (1/2 cup) butter, at room temperature
3/4 cup plus 1/2 teaspoon sugar
6 eggs, separated
2 teaspoons freshly grated orange peel
3 tablespoons Grand Marnier
1/8 teaspoon salt
1/8 teaspoon cream of tartar
Chocolate Cream (following)

In the top pan of a double boiler melt chocolate over hot water and let cool to room temperature. Mix nuts with flour. In a large mixing bowl beat butter and 3/4 cup sugar until creamy and beat in egg yolks. Mash orange peel with 1/2 teaspoon sugar to bring out its oils. Stir into yolk mixture melted chocolate, half the nut-flour mixture, orange peel, and Grand Marnier. Beat egg whites until foamy, add salt and cream of tartar and beat until stiff, glossy peaks form. Fold one-third of the whites into the chocolate-yolk mixture to lighten it, then gently fold in remaining whites along with remaining nut-flour mixture. Pour into a buttered and floured 9-inch spring-form pan. Bake in a 350° F. oven for 30 to 35 minutes, or until a toothpick inserted in the center comes out clean. Let cool for 10 minutes on a wire rack, then remove from pan. Let cool completely, then spoon poufs of Chocolate Cream on top of cake and serve remaining cream in a bowl alongside. Makes 16 servings.

CHOCOLATE CREAM Whip 1 cup whipping cream until stiff and mix in 3 tablespoons sweetened chocolate powder, 1 tablespoon powdered sugar, and 1 tablespoon Grand Marnier.

CHOCOLATE–GLAZED RASPBERRY TORTE

1 can (8 ounces) almond paste
6 eggs, separated
1/2 cup sugar
1-1/2 tablespoons fresh lemon juice
1 teaspoon freshly grated lemon peel
1/2 cup all-purpose flour
3/4 teaspoon baking powder
2/3 cup raspberry jelly
6 ounces semisweet chocolate
3 tablespoons butter
3 tablespoons sliced almonds

Place almond paste in a mixing bowl, add egg yolks, one at a time, and beat after each addition until smooth. Beat in 1/4 cup of the sugar and the lemon juice and peel. Beat egg whites until soft peaks form, add remaining 1/4 cup sugar and beat until stiff, glossy peaks form. Fold one-third of egg whites into yolk mixture to lighten it, then gently fold in remaining whites. Stir together the flour and baking powder, sprinkle over the egg mixture, and gently fold in. Butter two 9-inch round cake pans, line bottoms of pans with waxed paper, and then butter and flour the waxed paper. Divide batter evenly between the prepared pans. Bake in a 350° F. oven for 30 to 35 minutes, or until golden brown and a toothpick inserted in center comes out clean. Let cakes cool 5 minutes, then remove from pans and cool on racks.

To assemble, place 1 layer on a serving platter. Heat raspberry jelly until melted and spread over the layer; top with remaining layer. In the top pan of a double boiler combine chocolate and butter and melt over hot water, stirring to blend. With a spatula spread chocolate mixture on top and sides of cake. Sprinkle almonds around the outer edge of the top. Chill to set. Makes 16 servings.

CHOCOLATE–SHEATHED RUM PRALINE CAKE

Two 9-inch Sponge Cake
  layers (following)
Rum Syrup (following)
Chocolate Butter Cream
  (following)
Praline (following)
1 cup whipping cream

Prepare the Sponge Cake layers. Spoon over Rum Syrup and let cool. Prepare the Chocolate Butter Cream and Praline. Whip cream until stiff and fold in half the Praline. Spread one cake layer with half the whipped-cream mixture. Top with second layer and spread with remaining whipped-cream mixture. Frost sides of cake with Chocolate Butter Cream and sprinkle top with remaining Praline. Makes 12 servings.

SPONGE CAKE Separate 6 eggs. Beat the egg whites until foamy, add 1/8 teaspoon each salt and cream of tartar, and beat until soft peaks form. Gradually adding 1/4 cup sugar, beat until stiff, glossy peaks form. Beat the 6 egg yolks and 1 tablespoon fresh lemon juice until thick and lemon-colored, then gradually beat in 3/4 cup sugar. Fold one-third of egg whites into yolk mixture to lighten it, then gently fold in remaining whites. Butter two 9-inch round cake pans, line bottoms with waxed paper, and then butter and flour waxed paper. Divide batter evenly between prepared pans. Bake in a 350° F.

oven for 25 to 30 minutes, or until golden brown and tops spring back when touched. Let cool on wire rack, then turn out of pans. Makes two 9-inch layers.

CHOCOLATE BUTTER CREAM In the top pan of a double boiler melt 4 ounces semi-sweet chocolate over hot water; let cool. Beat 4 tablespoons (1/4 cup) butter, at room temperature, until creamy, and mix in 1/2 cup powdered sugar and 1/2 teaspoon vanilla extract. Stir in melted chocolate and blend well.

RUM SYRUP Heat 1/4 cup sugar and 1/4 cup water in a saucepan, stirring until sugar dissolves. Remove from heat and stir in 3 tablespoons rum.

PRALINE Heat 1/2 cup sugar in a heavy skillet over medium-high heat until sugar melts and caramelizes. Add 1/2 cup chopped almonds or hazelnuts and shake pan to coat nuts with syrup. Turn out of pan onto a sheet of buttered foil. Let cool. Pulverize in a blender. Store in a jar tightly covered if made in advance.

SERVES TWENTY PERSONS

Frozen Chocolate Macaroon Mousse
Frozen Raspberry Mousse
Frozen Grand Marnier Mousse
Truffles, Thin Mints, and Salted Nuts
Framboise Champagne
Coffee and Tea (optional)

Dessert Shower Party

A trio of frozen Italian-style mousses in assorted colors makes a bewitching dessert spread for a shower party. Accompany with champagne tinted pale pink with raspberry juice for a chic beverage to match the occasion.

SHOPPING LIST Purchase the ingredients for the mousses, plus candies and nuts.

COOK AHEAD Freeze the mousses as long as two weeks in advance, or make them at least a day ahead of time.

SERVING LOGISTICS As a prelude to dessert, offer the Framboise Champagne, candy, and nuts during gift-opening time. Later, set out the frozen mousses on a buffet, each sliced, so guests may help themselves to one or all. One has the option of making large frozen tortes to slice at serving time, or making individual mousses in fluted foil cupcake papers for easy serving. This party plan will serve twenty guests with ease. For a smaller group, prepare just one or two tortes.

FROZEN GRAND MARNIER MOUSSE

1-1/3 cups plus 1 tablespoon sugar
1/3 cup water
8 egg yolks
1 tablespoon freshly grated orange peel
3 cups whipping cream
1/4 cup Grand Marnier
Toasted slivered almonds or cocoa powder

Combine 1-1/3 cups sugar and water in a small pan. Bring to a boil and boil until the temperature reaches 238° F. on a candy thermometer (soft-ball stage). Meanwhile, beat egg yolks with an electric mixer until thick and pale yellow. Continuing to beat yolks, slowly pour hot syrup over them in a fine, steady stream. Beat until mixture cools to room temperature, about 7 minutes. Mash orange peel with 1 tablespoon sugar to bring out its oils; stir into the yolk mixture. Whip cream until stiff and beat in Grand Marnier. Fold into the yolk mixture. Spoon into a 9- or 10-inch spring-form pan. Cover and freeze until firm. To serve, remove pan sides and place on a platter. Garnish with almonds or sprinkle cocoa powder through a wire strainer, dusting top lightly. Makes 12 servings.

NOTE If desired, spoon mousse into fluted foil cupcake papers placed in a muffin pan. Makes about 12 individual mousses.

FROZEN CHOCOLATE MACAROON MOUSSE

1-1/4 cups sugar
1/3 cup water
1 teaspoon light corn syrup
4 egg whites
8 ounces semisweet chocolate
1/2 cup double-strength coffee
1 teaspoon vanilla extract
1-1/2 cups whipping cream
1/4 cup coffee-flavored
  liqueur or Cointreau
12 almond macaroons

Combine the sugar, water, and corn syrup in a small pan. Bring to a boil and boil over high heat until the temperature reaches 238° F. on a candy thermometer (soft-ball stage). Meanwhile, beat egg whites with an electric mixer until soft peaks form, then gradually beat in the hot syrup. Continue beating at high speed until mixture cools to room temperature.

Combine chocolate and coffee in the top pan of a double boiler placed over hot water, and heat until melted, stirring to blend. Let cool, stir in vanilla extract, and fold into the egg-white mixture. Whip cream until stiff, stir in 2 tablespoons of the liqueur, and fold in the chocolate mixture. Spoon chocolate mousse into a 9- or 10-inch spring-form pan. Dip macaroons in remaining liqueur to moisten lightly and arrange on top. Cover and freeze until firm. To serve, remove pan sides, place on a platter, and cut in wedges. Makes 12 servings.

NOTE If desired, spoon mousse into fluted foil cupcake papers placed in a muffin pan, and top each with crumbled macaroons that have been saturated with liqueur. Makes about 12 individual servings.

FROZEN RASPBERRY MOUSSE

1-1/4 cups sugar
1/3 cup water
1 teaspoon light corn syrup
4 egg whites
2 packages (10 ounces *each*)
  frozen raspberries, thawed
2 cups whipping cream
Chocolate curls or raspberries
  (optional)

Combine the sugar, water, and corn syrup in a small pan. Bring to a boil and boil until the temperature reaches 238° F. on a candy thermometer (soft-ball stage). Meanwhile, beat egg whites with an electric mixer until soft peaks form, then gradually beat in the hot syrup; continue beating at high speed until mixture cools to room temperature. Purée raspberries in a blender and press through a wire sieve, discarding seeds. Fold purée into egg whites. Whip cream until stiff and fold in. Spoon mousse into a 9- or 10-inch spring-form pan. Cover and freeze until firm. To serve, remove pan sides, place on a platter, and cut in wedges. If desired, garnish with chocolate curls or raspberries. Makes 12 servings.

NOTE If desired, spoon mousse into fluted foil cupcake papers placed in a muffin pan. Makes about 12 individual mousses.

SERVES TWENTY–FOUR TO THIRTY–SIX PERSONS

Vanilla Bean Ice Cream
Coffee Bean Ice Cream
Grand Marnier Ice Cream, Italian Style
Peach Ice Cream
Strawberry Ice
Lemon Ice

Ice-Cream-Cranking Party

In the summertime a home-made-ice cream party is a delight for both children and adults. A group of friends or neighbors can turn out a tantalizing array of ice creams and ices with three or four ice cream makers, either crank style or electric. The quintet of flavors presented here is delicious to savor in small spoonfuls served together in bowls or big paper cups, Italian fashion. Or if desired, churn only one or two kinds.

SHOPPING LIST Purchase the ingredients for the ice cream recipes.

COOK AHEAD The ice cream bases are best made several hours in advance and refrigerated. Or make them a day ahead.

SERVING LOGISTICS Informality is the key to this convivial party. Guests may wish to savor the ice creams while still soft from churning. Or allow them to firm up and the flavors to mellow for an hour before serving.

VANILLA BEAN ICE CREAM

4 egg yolks
3/4 cup sugar
2 cups (1 pint) half-and-half
   cream
1 vanilla bean, or 2 teaspoons
   vanilla extract
2 cups whipping cream
Crushed ice and rock salt
   for churning

Beat egg yolks slightly in the top pan of a double boiler and stir in sugar and half-and-half cream. Split vanilla bean and scrape its seeds into the cream and add the bean as well. Place over simmering water and stirring constantly, cook until mixture is custardlike and coats the spoon. Remove from heat and refrigerate until cold, or for several hours if possible. Remove vanilla bean. If using vanilla extract, stir in at this point.

Just before ready to churn, stir in whipping cream, then pour into a 2-quart ice cream freezer can. Place filled can in freezer pail and adjust dasher. Pack crushed ice and rock salt around can in the proportion of five parts ice to one part salt. Churn (using the crank or electric motor) until ice cream is frozen. At this point it will become difficult to crank or the motor will labor. Allow 15 to 25 minutes. Remove dasher, scrape ice cream back into can, and cover can. Drain off excess salt water and repack with ice and salt to hold until ready to serve. Makes about 1-3/4 quarts.

COFFEE BEAN ICE CREAM

Follow the basic recipe for Vanilla Bean Ice Cream, preceding, omitting vanilla bean and reducing vanilla extract to 1 teaspoon. In addition, dissolve 1/3 cup instant freeze-dried coffee in 3 tablespoons hot water. Let cool and stir into the basic custard mixture with vanilla extract. Freeze as directed. Makes about 1-3/4 quarts.

PEACH ICE CREAM

Follow the basic recipe for Vanilla Bean Ice Cream, preceding, omitting vanilla bean or extract and using only 1 cup half-and-half cream. Stir 2 cups puréed peaches, sweetened to taste, and 2 tablespoons fresh lemon juice into the cool custard. Freeze as directed. Makes about 2 quarts.

GRAND MARNIER ICE CREAM, ITALIAN STYLE

3/4 cup plus 2 teaspoons
   sugar
1 tablespon light corn syrup
1/4 cup water
5 egg yolks
2 teaspoons freshly grated
   orange peel
2 cups whipping cream
1-3/4 cups half-and-half cream
1/4 cup Grand Marnier

Combine 3/4 cup sugar, corn syrup, and water in a small pan. Bring to a boil and boil until the temperature reaches 238° F. on a candy thermometer (soft-ball stage). Meanwhile, beat egg yolks with an electric mixer until thick and pale yellow. Continuing to beat yolks, slowly pour in the sugar syrup in a fine, steady stream. Beat until the mixture cools to room temperature, about 7 minutes. When cool, refrigerate mixture until cold, or for several hours if possible.

Mash orange peel with 2 teaspoons sugar to bring out its oils and stir into chilled mixture with whipping cream, half-and-half cream, and Grand Marnier. Pour into a 2-quart ice cream freezer can. Place filled can in freezer pail and adjust dasher. Pack crushed ice and rock salt around can in the proportion of five parts ice to one part salt. Churn (using the crank or electric motor) until ice cream is frozen. At this point it will become difficult to crank or the motor will labor. Allow 15 to 25 minutes. Remove dasher, scrape ice cream back into can, and cover can. Drain off excess salt water and repack with ice and salt to hold until ready to serve. Makes about 1-3/4 quarts.

STRAWBERRY ICE

6 cups strawberry purée
  (about 2-1/2 quarts berries)
2/3 cup sugar
2 tablespoons fresh lemon
  juice

Combine the berry purée, sugar, and lemon juice, stir well to dissolve sugar, and chill thoroughly. Pour into a 2-quart ice cream freezer can. Place filled can in freezer pail and adjust dasher. Pack crushed ice and rock salt around can in the proportion of five parts ice to one part salt. Churn (using the crank or electric motor) until the ice is frozen. At this point it will become difficult to crank or the motor will labor. Allow 15 to 25 minutes. Remove dasher, scrape the ice back into can, and cover can. Drain off excess salt water and repack with ice and salt to hold until ready to serve. Makes about 2 quarts.

LEMON ICE

2 cups plus 1 tablespoon
  sugar
3 cups water
1 tablespoons freshly grated
  lemon peel
1-1/2 cups fresh lemon juice

Combine 2 cups sugar and the water in a saucepan and bring to a boil, stirring to dissolve sugar. Cook until syrup is clear. Meanwhile, mash orange peel with 1 tablespoon sugar to bring out its oils. Remove syrup from heat and stir in lemon peel and juice. Let cool and chill thoroughly. Freeze as directed for Strawberry Ice, preceding. Makes about 1-3/4 quarts.

Index

LOU SEIBERT PAPPAS is the food editor of the *Peninsula Times Tribune* in Palo Alto, California. A former food consultant for *Sunset* magazine, she now writes for *Gourmet* and *Cuisine* magazines and is the author of a dozen other cookbooks, including *International Fish Cookery* and *Egg Cookery* published by 101 Productions. She has made eleven extensive tours to Europe collecting recipes and ideas for her books. She and her husband, Nicholas, have three sons and a daughter.

VERONICA DI ROSA is a graduate of Vancouver School of Art, and later opened Canada's first kitchen shop. After coming to the United States, she produced three unusual single-recipe books—*Chocolate Decadence, Sinful Strawberries* and *Virtuous Vanilla*—with chef Janice Feuer. She has also illustrated two other 101 cookbooks: *Sweets for Saints and Sinners* and *Flavors of Mexico*. She lives in the Napa Valley with her husband, vineyardist Rene di Rosa.